Psychology and the Black Experience

Contemporary Psychology Series
Edward L. Walker, Editor

The frontiers of psychology are advancing—advancing in response to persistent and fundamental social problems, advancing as a result of improved technology in both research and application, advancing through individual creative effort.

Brooks/Cole Publishing Company will make contemporary ideas, research, and applications widely available to students and scholars through the Contemporary Psychology Series.

Psychological Aspects of International Conflict
  Ross Stagner, Wayne State University

An Anatomy for Conformity
  Edward L. Walker, The University of Michigan
  Roger W. Heyns, President, American Council on Education

Delinquent Behavior in an American City
  Martin Gold, The University of Michigan

Feminine Personality and Conflict
  Judith M. Bardwick, The University of Michigan
  Elizabeth Douvan, The University of Michigan
  Matina Horner, Harvard University
  David Gutmann, The University of Michigan

Roles Women Play: Readings Toward Women's Liberation
  Michele Hoffnung Garskof, Quinnipiac College

Homosexuality and Psychological Functioning
  Mark Freedman

Psychology and the Black Experience
  Roderick W. Pugh, Loyola University of Chicago

Psychology and the Black Experience

Roderick W. Pugh
Loyola University of Chicago

with contributions by

Thomas J. Edwards
LaMaurice H. Gardner
Norman G. Kerr

Brooks/Cole Publishing Company
Monterey, California
A Division of Wadsworth Publishing Company, Inc.
Belmont, California

© 1972 by Wadsworth Publishing Company, Inc., Belmont, California 94002. All rights reserved. No part of this book may be reproduced, stored in a retrieval system, or transcribed, in any form or by any means—electronic, mechanical, photocopying, recording, or otherwise—without the prior written permission of the publisher: Brooks/Cole Publishing Company, Monterey, California, a division of Wadsworth Publishing Company, Inc.

ISBN: 0-8185-0059-X
L.C. Catalog Card No: 72-80674
Printed in the United States of America
1 2 3 4 5 6 7 8 9 10—77 76 75 74 73 72

This book was edited by Anne Phillips and designed by Linda Marcetti. It was typeset by Holmes Typography, Inc., San Jose, California, and printed and bound by Malloy Lithographing, Inc., Ann Arbor, Michigan.

Preface

Psychology and the Black Experience grew out of a symposium by black psychologists that was sponsored by the Department of Psychology of Loyola University of Chicago in April, 1970. The succession of critical developments in this country during the 1960s generated a need on the part of Loyola students and faculty to understand the nature of the black experience, to examine the significance of black activism, and to explore at least some aspects of a relationship that professional psychology might have to these. Who might better address themselves to such issues than a panel of black professional psychologists? The responsibility for organizing and chairing such a symposium fell to me. The symposium participants were Doris W. Welcher of Johns Hopkins University and the three contributors to this work, Thomas J. Edwards, LaMaurice H. Gardner, and Norman G. Kerr.

Each of the first six chapters may be read and appreciated individually, but they pair off conveniently into three groups, which form the parts into which the volume is divided. Part One (Chapters One and Two) consists of a psychological assessment of the Black Revolution and an examination of one of its important wings, black student activism. These two chapters together present a philosophical and psychological frame of reference related to the better understanding and appreciation of the four chapters and Epilogue that follow.

Part Two focuses on the particular professional concerns of two black clinical psychologists. One specializes in psychoanalytically oriented psychotherapy with individual clients, and the other is engaged in organizing mental health services for a large urban black community. These are diverse aspects of what psychologists refer to as professional intervention. Chapter Three, Part Two, deals with classical psychotherapeutic intervention and is the most technical of the essays. Chapter Four, Part Two, examines the philosophy, methods, and difficulties associated with devising an effective community psychology program for urban blacks.

Human behavior in the context of life's experiences is the ultimate concern of psychology. Chapters Five and Six, Part Three, are autobiographical recollections from the lives of two black professional psychologists. These accounts serve to illustrate concretely the nature of the black experience and the struggle for personal integrity, which is the critical challenge for the black person in the context of American society, regardless of his socioeconomic background or achievement potential. Such are the circumstances and individual experiences that give rise to all the issues identified and examined in the first four chapters.

The concluding chapter is in some respects an epilogue (Chapter Seven). It treats briefly the issue of a "black psychology" and presents five principles that are necessary to guarantee continued black psychological survival.

The reader's attention is called to the rather extensive glossary of terms, which has been added specifically to make this volume more useful for the layman to psychology. It also defines army terms mentioned in Chapter Six.

I wish to thank Drs. Gardner, Kerr, and Edwards for consenting to have their symposium presentations become a part of this volume as Chapters Three, Four, and Five. I wrote the other chapters specifically for this publication; they were not a part of the original symposium. Dr. Frank J. Kobler and Dr. Ronald E. Walker deserve special mention for the symposium idea as well as for lending every support to its success. The symposium was funded in part by a United States Public Health Training Grant in Clinical Psychology No. MH 10890-03. I also want to thank the E. B. Marks Music Corporation for permission to reprint lyrics from "Lift Ev'ry Voice and Sing." Appreciation also goes to the members of Psi Chi, the national honor society in psychology, for their interest and assistance with the symposium. Finally, much gratitude goes to Edward L. Walker, Janice Nelson, James Futterer, Patrick Shields, and Nancy McCool, whose assistance was invaluable in many ways either with the symposium or with the preparation of this volume.

Roderick W. Pugh

Contents

Part One
A Black Psychologist Interprets the Black Revolution   1

    1. The Black Revolution: The Psychology of Self-Reclamation   3
    2. Black Student Activism   25

Part Two
Black Psychologists at Work   35

    3. Psychotherapy under Varying Conditions of Race– LaMaurice H. Gardner   37
    4. The Black Community's Challenge to Psychology– Norman G. Kerr   55

Part Three
From the Lives of Black Psychologists   63

    5. Looking Back on Growing Up Black– Thomas J. Edwards   65
    6. The Making and Breaking of a Black Soldier   73

Epilogue   101

    7. Black Psychological Survival   103

    Glossary   109
    Index   116

Notes about the Contributors

Thomas J. Edwards is Professor of Education and Director of the Learning Center, State University of New York at Buffalo. His special interest is in the effects of cultural differences on learning, and he was for five years Literacy Advisor to the Iranian Ministry of Education, Teheran, Iran. His Ph.D. is from Temple University.

LaMaurice H. Gardner is a Loyola University Ph.D. whose theoretical position is psychoanalytic. He is Director of the Children's Center of Wayne County, Michigan, in addition to being an Adjunct Associate Professor of Psychology at Wayne State University and an Adjunct Assistant Professor at the University of Detroit. He is a Diplomate of the American Board of Professional Psychology.

Norman G. Kerr specializes in mental health administration and community psychology. He is Director of the Malcolm X Shabazz Community Health Center, Chicago, and is Assistant Mental Health Superintendent of Manteno State Hospital. He is a Loyola University Ph.D. in psychology and a Diplomate of the American Board of Professional Psychology.

Part One

A Black Psychologist Interprets the Black Revolution

Chapter One
The Black Revolution: The Psychology of Self-Reclamation

I have awakened from the unknowing to the knowing hoping to see the fathomless ... [Latimer, 1949, p. 208].

What Is the Black Revolution?

We are now in the early phase of the most constructive social development of modern times in these United States of America. This social development promises to be one of the most significant and far-reaching of contemporary civilization. It is born out of the American black man's will to survive, his will to overcome the effects of radical oppression, and his will to achieve self-actualization. It is called the Black Revolution.

As most social developments are, the Black Revolution is highly complex and must be properly understood in relation to its historical antecedents and its historical context. It is influenced by—and in turn influences—national and world history, politics, and cultural evolution. Its complexity allows it to be viewed or interpreted from many vantage points, all of which have a certain validity. The Revolution is often thought of in terms of its specific goals, such as social, educational, economic, and political enhancement in local and world society. These practical end-purposes of the Revolution are given different priorities by different factions of the national black community.

Sometimes the Revolution is characterized by its tactics, strategies, or methods. It is described as violent, nonviolent, or disposed to employ "whatever means necessary" to achieve its purposes. Such descriptions generally reflect the degree of "militancy" of the particular advocate.

Chrisman (1970) is among those who, in assessing the meaning of the Black Revolution, tend to emphasize its cultural and political aspects. He states:

> The black revolution is both a cultural revolution and a political revolution, and each enforces the other. Politics is a cultural act and culture is a political fact. For culture is the collective thrust of a people and it encompasses the economic, political, social, and esthetic conditions of their existence [p. 6].

One would hardly argue with the general validity of this assessment, but it fails to call attention to the basic process of human behavior on which the Black Revolution rests.

Psychological Factors Are Central to the Black Revolution

It is the thesis of this essay that the basic elements of the Black Revolution are psychological. It is the psychological vantage point that focuses on the individual and group processes of evolving experience, awareness, understanding, sense-of-self, motivation, goal direction, and action that explains the Revolution. I will attempt to identify and assess the principal psychological factors that are basic to the Revolution as a process of human behavior.

One of the earliest published statements that grasped the essential psychology of the Black Revolution was the following by Carmichael and Hamilton (1967):

> Black people must redefine themselves, and only *they* can do that. Throughout this country, vast segments of the black communities are beginning to recognize the need to assert their own definitions, to reclaim their history, their culture; to create their own sense of community and togetherness. There is a growing resentment of the word "Negro," for example, because this term is the invention of our oppressor; it is *his* image of us that he describes. Many blacks are now calling themselves African-Americans, Afro-Americans or black people

because that is *our* image of ourselves. When we begin to define our own image, ... the black community will have a positive image of itself that *it* has created [p. 37].

Nathan Hare (1971) restates these principles, reflecting the trend since 1967 toward a more militant and nationalistically political stance by an increasingly large segment of the black community:

I am an African: I am the exotic quintessence of a universal blackness, an unbreakable link between my past victimization and the inevitable resurgence of an ancient and glorious history, an eternal pastness. I have lost by force my land, my language, my life. I will seize it again, so help me, but this will never be fully accomplished until I have restored the integrity of my race [p. 35].

Morris (1969) defines revolution as "an assertedly momentous change in any situation ... [p. 1113]." The Black Revolution is the "assertedly momentous change" in the American black people's reassertion of themselves as persons and as a people. It is the relatively sudden emergence of changed attitudes and behavior resulting from a reintegration of a sense-of-self which has been painfully long in the making.

Black people collectively are now rejecting the most insidious and debilitating effect of more than 300 years of racial oppression in this country. *This has been a deeply instilled sense of self-devaluation and inferiority, with its accompanying pervasive insecurity and inhibition of self-actualizing assertion.* Black people are again wresting for themselves a legitimate self-concept and sense of self-esteem. The revolutionary impact of this development on black people as well as the overall society derives not merely from the nature of this reintegrative process per se, but also from the *degree of dedication* to it. Although it is toward life that they strive, black people have demonstrated to themselves and to the world that they are, if need be, willing to put their lives on the line in order to insure authentic life for those who will survive. They no longer passively submit to the noose of the lynch mob or to any of the less obvious but more insidious evidences of white racism. Thus, these two psychological processes are hypothesized as constituting the basis and essence of the Black Revolution: (1) a reintegration of self-concept (individual and group); and (2) a high degree of motivation (drive, dedication) toward achieving concrete goals at every level of living that support self-actualization and a constructive reintegration of self-concept.

The Birth of the Black Revolution

When did the Black Revolution come into being? Again, a designated time for its realization might depend largely on one's frame of reference, whether historical, economic, political, or psychological. The seeds of the Black Revolution were planted in the early seventeenth century on the day the first slaves were sold to traders on the west coast of Africa. From then it developed from a long evolutionary network of interrelated and reactive processes. However, on the basis of the present thesis that the central elements of the Revolution are psychological, one might ask when it was that the psychological factors of the Revolution coalesced, thus heralding the recognizable birth of the Revolution. It happened during the great summer of discontent when blacks en masse demanded *full citizenship* in this country with *all* the rights *now* and *all* the privileges *now* appertaining thereto. The Black Revolution was born on August 28, 1963, in the nation's capitol. The event was the March on Washington.

The March on Washington of 1963 is selected as symbolizing the psychological birth of the Black Revolution because no other single event is so responsible for crystallizing a national sense of black unity, identity, pride, and dedication to a commonness of purpose.

> It was a day to be remembered ... It was a day of pride and of dignity. It was a day of rededication to the struggle for freedom now. It was an historic day ["A Day to Remember," 1963, p. 466].

Even though the March was an integrated (multigroup, multiracial) effort, the leadership and superstars of the demonstration were outstandingly black. This fact alone was history-making. Blacks had never before so impressively asserted their own leadership for all the nation and the world to witness. From that day on it was unmistakably evident that American blacks would drop the passive stance and pursue their own destiny as a people under their own leadership. In spite of the superleader of the day, Martin Luther King, and his "I Have a Dream" speech, which captured the emotional revival of that historic moment, it was also evident that the leadership was not ultimately centered in one person or vested in one faction.

The March on Washington was a surprise success to most American blacks. Had most blacks dreamed that it would be the success that it was, the demonstrators might have numbered two to three times the 250,000 ("A Day to Remember," 1963) who were actually present.

Until that day, blacks were still laboring under the self-debasing stereotype that they could never depend on each other to cooperate in any massive effort for their mutual benefit; many did not want to go all the way to Washington to participate in a flop. However, the notion that blacks could not cooperate among themselves had been progressively undermined in the minds of blacks by the success of such organized efforts as the Montgomery bus boycott of 1955, the sit-ins of 1960, the freedom rides of 1961, and the black-white confrontations in Birmingham of 1963 (see Table 1–1).

Table 1–1
The birth of the Black Revolution
and related historical events, 1954–1968.

Date	Event
1954	Supreme Court school desegregation decision.
1955, Dec.	Rosa Parks refused to sit in the back of the bus: The Montgomery, Alabama, bus boycott began.
1957	Southern Christian Leadership Conference (SCLC) founded by Martin Luther King, Jr.
1957, Sept.	Little Rock incident: Eisenhower sent federal troops to guarantee school integration.
1960, Feb.	Sit-ins began in Greensboro, North Carolina.
1960, Nov.	John Kennedy elected President (assumed office January, 1961).
1961, May	Freedom rides began.
1962, Sept.	James Meredith admitted as first black student to University of Mississippi.
1963, Apr.–May	Black-white confrontation, Birmingham, Alabama.
1963, June	Medgar Evers assassinated in Mississippi.
1963, Aug.	*March on Washington: The psychological birth of the Black Revolution.*
1963, Nov.	John Kennedy assassinated in Dallas, Texas.
1964, July	Massive civil rights legislation signed into law by Lyndon Johnson.
1964–1967	Ghetto riots, Rochester, 1964; Los Angeles, 1965; Chicago, 1965; Cleveland, 1966; Detroit, 1967; Newark, 1967.
1965, Feb.	Malcolm X assassinated, New York City.
1965, Mar.	Black-white confrontation in Selma, Alabama.
1965, Aug.	Voting rights legislation signed into law by Lyndon Johnson.
1965–1967	Southern drive for voter registration by SCLC and other civil rights organizations.
1968, Apr.	Martin Luther King assassinated in Memphis, Tennessee.
1968, June	Robert Kennedy assassinated in Los Angeles, California.

In addition, the heroic, self-sacrificing bravery and dedication of such individuals as Rosa Parks of Montgomery, the black students of Little Rock, and above all James Meredith and Medgar Evers of Mississippi had moved every black in the country to reassess his notions about his people and his dedication to the common cause of his people. A sufficient number had been so moved that they went to Washington and created on that August day in 1963 perhaps the greatest single corrective learning experience for a people in all history. On that day many blacks were proud to be black for the first time. Pride in blackness and mutual faith and confidence among black people has grown with acceleration ever since that day.

The Black Revolution and Black Liberation

A few weeks ago a white colleague of mine asked in all sincerity what it means when Negroes nowadays talk about "liberation." He said he was puzzled by this, because—as bad as things might still be for Negroes—certainly they were no longer slaves in need of liberation! This reaction was all the more meaningful because it came from a knowledgeable white person with extensive exposure to people and conditions in both the South and the North, a person who is "liberal" in his thinking and in his politics and rejects racism. Yet, because he views the situation from the white perspective and not the black, it is not easy for him to understand that in reality black people are still unliberated.

Black people are not yet liberated in this country because the psychological processes basic to the Black Revolution have not achieved closure: the reintegration of self-concept is not yet complete for the totality of the national black community, and the drive toward achieving support for this reintegration at every level of experience has not been satisfied. The self-actualizing goals of the Revolution, summarized by Carmichael and Hamilton (1967) as black people achieving " ... full participation in the decision-making processes affecting the lives of black people ... [p. 47]," are far from being realized. These are minimum requirements for liberation.

Otherwise stated, liberation is the freedom to be one's self fully as a human being, with all aspects of one's developmental, educational, social, political, and cultural experiences supporting that freedom. When black people can fully embrace a sense of identity and self-acceptance based on criteria emanating from blackness rather than from whiteness, and when they can be essentially in charge of their own lives and free from a controlling and oppressive dependency in society, then they will be liberated. When and by what means this ideal will be achieved is yet another question.

A Summary Look at the Case History

History and Behaving Individuals

In recent years, under the impact of the Black Revolution, there has been a renewed interest in the history of blacks in this country. Over and above genetically endowed characteristics and capacities, people are made by their history. The history of a people consists of the collective ongoing experiences of the group and of the individual members of the group.

People are products of their history; but as they live, grow, and act, they in turn influence their history. Therefore, there is an interesting interaction between ongoing experience (history) and the acting, behaving person. The less knowledgeable people are about the circumstances in which they find themselves and the less power they have in those circumstances, the less likely they are to influence their experiences (history) in the directions that they might desire. For example, the experiences of an infant are largely determined by adults with power, whereas the adult with greater comprehension and power is in a much better position to determine the nature of his own experiences. However, the adult is most likely to influence his ongoing experiences in ways determined by what he has learned from his past experiences.

Blacks were transported to this country under conditions that determined their having little comprehension of Western civilization in the process of industrialization, and the total circumstances of their slavery. In addition, they were completely powerless. Suicide was about the only power option left to the individual slave. Therefore, in those years after the first slaves landed in 1619, the directive influence that blacks had on their own experiences was relatively insignificant. It was not until two centuries later that the ability to influence their own experiences as a collective group had grown relatively more significant, as evidenced by the lives of Nat Turner, Charles Remond (the first prominent black abolitionist), and Frederick Douglass (Bennett, 1962).

From the beginning there was sporadic overt resistance against slavery on the part of individuals and small groups of blacks, but by the first half of the nineteenth century black resistance was beginning to be more sophisticated and threatening. Some blacks were beginning to show a useful comprehension of the alien culture and the circumstances of their bondage. This led to rudimentary attempts at the development of power—attempts at systematic, organized resistance.

At that stage of history, however, only a relatively small number of blacks were openly involved in such action. A large percentage of blacks, out of ignorance, fear, and an *adaptive inferiority*, believed that their plight was no more than they should expect or even deserve (!), and so they were basically accepting of their condition. There was generalized identification with the aggressor, and the form of resistance—when present—was largely passive.

Anxiety Conditioned to Blackness

Until the Black Revolution took form, hardly any experience of a black person in this society authentically supported his sense of self-worth *as a black person*. Some experiences may have supported his sense of worth as a good nigger slave, as a preacher, as a cook, as a schoolteacher, as a pimp, as a hard worker, as an athlete, as an entertainer, as a student, or as a parent, but not as a *black person*. One was a "good this" or a "good that" *in spite of* being black. One's blackness was always there to detract from a feeling of complete well-being and congruence of self. It was always there, either at a conscious or unconscious level, demanding to be dealt with. It was there decreasing one's personal acceptability because that was the constant feedback blacks received from the white majority from the beginning of their mutual history in this country. In time this was the feedback blacks learned to give themselves as if to confirm a self-fulfilling prophecy.

What was the nature of the original black experience—the nature of the first feedback? It is now very difficult to conceive of how total the exploitation of blacks was during slavery. A slave was presented with only two alternatives: life under conditions of total exploitation—physical, sexual, and emotional—or death. Many blacks chose death, and those who chose life did so at *extreme psychological expense*. Grier and Cobbs (1968) present a brilliant elaboration of the psychology of the black experience in their book *Black Rage*—a book that in my opinion is " . . . a giant step towards a definitive psychological interpretation of the relationship between black and white in this country [Pugh, 1969, p. 296]." Grier and Cobbs emphasize that the despising of blacks has been a unique element in the national character of this country, and that because of this " . . . the overriding experience of the black American has been grief and sorrow and no man can change that fact [p. 209]."

Until very recently blacks in this country have been considered fair game in a 12-month open season. I can still recall the helpless dread I felt as a small child when the Ku Klux Klan paraded in my birthplace, Richmond, Kentucky, and burned their huge crosses draped with rubber tires. We stood transfixed in rigid silence as they marched by, realizing that our lives depended on the whim of any one of them; we were without recourse. Any notion of equal protection under the law was a mockery. We were governed daily by the knowledge that the "penalty for misjudging a situation involving white men . . . [would be] . . . death [Grier and Cobbs, 1968, p. 208]."

The era of lynching, which stretched essentially from the emancipation to the 1920s, was a reign of terror for black people. Lerone Bennett (1962) cites a report by W. E. B. DuBois that 1700 Negroes were lynched between 1885 and 1894 and that while DuBois attended Atlanta University, which was around 1901, " . . . an average of one Negro was lynched every week [p. 280]." Katz (1967, p. 344) confirms this count by stating that between 1892 and 1901, lynchings occurred at the rate of three to four a week. In 1892 there were 161 lynchings (Kerner, 1968, p. 216). By 1913 the estimate had dropped to 79 and was down to 38 in 1917, but it rose to 83 by 1919, the year after World War I. In that same year, 11 different Negroes were burned alive in 6 different states (Bennett, 1962). Of those lynched during the year after the "war to save democracy," a "substantial number" were black soldiers not yet out of uniform (Kerner, p. 219).

In the minds of blacks there was one thing and one thing only that was responsible for their being terrorized, slaughtered, segregated, and oppressed—their blackness. *Anxiety was conditioned to one's blackness.* This was a simple and easy association for people to make who were exposed to few contradictory experiences and who had been held by law to illiteracy, ignorance, and superstition as slaves. One cannot minimize the force of ignorance nor forget how painstakingly slow the first blacks began to acquire significant education and sophistication after the precedent of laws forbidding the education of slaves. Corrective emotional learning regarding blackness and anxiety associated with blackness is still in progress in 1972.

Adaptive Inferiority

Personality theory, especially that of Rogers (1961), stresses the necessity of achieving congruence if one is to be a fully functioning and well-adjusted individual. A state of congruence exists when all "systems" of personality organization are "go," so to speak. This means that all aspects of personality organization are functioning well in a mutually supportive way. If there is an aspect of personality that does not function well with or contribute constructively to the overall personality organization, then the functioning efficiency of the personality is decreased or perhaps even seriously disrupted.

Under these circumstances, the individual has two kinds of solutions available to him, broadly speaking. One kind is only a quasi-solution: it is to institute some psychological stopgap measures that at best minimize or compensate for the lowered functioning. Such psychological stopgap measures will merely ease the anxiety and unsettling feelings that accompany disrupted functioning. The other kind of solution is truly corrective: it solves the problem at its source by modifying the disrupting factor in ways that restore the congruence of the self-system and promote the full functioning efficiency of the personality.

Adaptive inferiority, identification with the aggressor, the color-caste system, and the be-like-white success formula are all psychological stopgap measures. They are sham, quasi-solutions that at best placate and momentarily reduce anxiety, but they solve no problems at their source nor resolve any conflicts definitively.

Adaptive inferiority is a psychological defense which, under stress so extreme that survival itself is threatened, allows for relative intactness of functioning within a seemingly valid structure of experience. Adaptive inferiority is an easily instituted defense when there is no precedent for "equality" with the dominant group. It is much less likely to occur when there has been such a precedent.

In the seventeenth century (and even now) "equality" was all too easily gauged on the basis of the most superficial and immediately evident status and power criteria such as number and size, facility with a particular culture and its language(s), material possessions, and military-political power and influence. Therefore the black man, being on the low end of all these criteria, was easily brainwashed into believing that these factors were evidence for his natural inferiority, especially when he had experienced no precedent of equality with the white American majority. Likewise the white man, because of the reverse of these conditions for himself, believed that his natural superiority over the black man was proven.

Adaptive inferiority served to reduce the impact of the black man's inner conflicts and frustrations. If one's inferiority is naturally accepted as valid, then domination by one's "superior" and a lessened lot in life are much more easily rationalized and accepted. One's experiences then make more sense, and the intactness of one's functioning can be relatively maintained within the context of personal experiences.

When I was an undergraduate at Fisk University in Nashville, Tennessee, the white president of the university once expressed to some of us his puzzlement as to how we managed so well psychologically under circumstances of segregation and oppression. His attitude seemed to say, "I don't think I could do it; I don't think I could tolerate it." Possibly he could not have, because he viewed the situation from a background and precedent of experienced equality. We had never had such a background. (Niggers were niggers, and white folks were white folks; and niggers just had to accept their lot in life!)

Adaptive Inferiority in Action

The "We-ain't-ready" Syndrome

As recently as the mid-60s it was common to hear one black person proclaim on witnessing some negative stereotypic behavior on the part of another: "You see, we ain't ready!"—meaning not ready to be treated "like white folks" and to share equal rights with them. Another example of the "we-ain't-ready" syndrome was illustrated when one black professional exclaimed with joking irony to another who was moving into a newly available (to blacks) luxury high-rise apartment building: "Now you know no niggers need to live like this!"—meaning, as well as white folks live.

During the height of public interest in the pending 1964 civil rights legislation, a near-illiterate black man who had recently migrated from the South to the North was asked his opinion of the civil rights push in Congress. His reply in a long, slow drawl was, "I don't pay no 'tention to dat. I don't need no civil rights. Dat's only fo' people with money!" In addition to his adaptive inferiority, this man expressed some significant insight into the meaninglessness of the *right* to enjoy certain privileges without the money to afford them.

Some Objective Assessments

In the early 40s I conducted one of the first objective studies of the comparative psychological adjustment of black students in integrated and separate schools. The study attempted to assess the attitudes of blacks toward themselves (Pugh, 1941). Other early objective or semiobjective studies focusing on the psychological adjustment of blacks were those of Crowley (1932), Davis (1937), Gandy (1938), Gregg (1938), and Frazier (1940), the latter being one of five studies sponsored by The American Council on Education in Washington, D. C. All of these studies provided ample evidence of the negative, self-rejecting attitudes on the part of blacks toward themselves as individuals and as a group. However, *the strength of such attitudes varied and tended to be most deep-seated among the most oppressed.* Those whose oppression had been balanced by some positive experiences and opportunities for self-enhancement seemed much more *ambivalent* toward themselves and "the Negro." As a result of certain corrective experiences, their adaptive inferiority had been undermined to that extent, and consequently they were more noticeably in conflict. They were also more inclined to take further corrective action.

A reexamination of the most differentiating and the least differentiating items of a scale entitled "Attitude of Negroes Towards Negroes," which I used (Pugh, 1941, 1943), will serve to illustrate some of the specifics of the self-rejecting attitudes and the ambivalence of blacks toward themselves as of the early 40s. The most differentiating items on a scale are those that tend to generate the greatest division of opinion. For example, a significant number of subjects will agree with such items, but a significant number will also disagree with the same items. The least differentiating items on a scale are those that generate no meaningful division of opinion. Although the sample for which this particular questionnaire was used was small (122 black students drawn from both integrated and all-black high schools in Dayton and Columbus, Ohio), it was considered fairly representative of the black high school population of that time and that geographical section of the country. The sample was restricted because several school principals (white) refused to allow their black students to take the questionnaire.

The 5 most differentiating items out of 60 were:

31. We are inferior to white people because our forefathers were earlier savages and later slaves.
54. I have often felt inferior because I am a Negro.

28. We ought not to say anything whenever one of our race is killed illegally for fear of making the white man mad.
7. Because of differences in skin color and quality of hair, prejudice within the race is to be expected.
57. I feel more self-conscious when in the presence of important white people than when in the presence of important Negroes.

In 1972, one would hardly expect these items to generate a division of opinion among black high school students anywhere in the country.

The following were among the least differentiating items out of 60—that is, they tended to generate no significant division of opinion. The usual answer is indicated in parentheses following the item.

8. Negroes are more outstanding in sports than whites as proved by Joe Louis, Jesse Owens, and Henry Armstrong. (YES)
14. Because comedians like "Rochester" attain wide popularity among whites, they should be considered Negro leaders. (NO)
27. It would be a disgrace to the Negro race if Paul Robeson married a white woman. (YES)
34. The inferior members of our race bring down the prejudice of the white man against all of us. (YES)
5. We should expect full-blooded Negroes to become leaders of our race. (YES)

A comparative examination of these most differentiating and least differentiating items suggests a sharp ambivalence on the part of these black high school students toward "the Negro" and therefore toward themselves. A good number felt inferior to whites because their "forefathers were earlier savages and later slaves," but almost all agreed that blacks were more outstanding in sports than whites. This latter negation of felt inferiority would seem to be directly responsive to the specific corrective experience of identifying with the outstanding athletic achievements of Joe Louis, Jesse Owens, and others. The study suggested that although there was still a generalized feeling of inferiority to whites (items 31, 54, and 57), in specific areas there was significant contradiction of this, such as in athletics.

A division in group identity is strongly suggested. The response to item 34 implies that certain blacks were considered inferior to others. Clearly, many of these students felt that wherever there were differences in "skin color and quality of hair" (item 7), even within their own race, there would be prejudice. This feeling was related to the existence of a definite color-caste system among blacks, which was even tacitly recognized and supported by many whites. The widespread attitude on the part of many blacks and also many whites was that the closer a black approximated being white, the more acceptable he was. The ultimate hitch there was that in order to be *completely accepted* one had to be *completely white*! Therefore, the be-like-white success formula was no success formula at all, and the great promise held out to blacks by whites—especially by those whites most responsible for and interested in black education—turned out to be an empty promise indeed. Nevertheless the be-like-white success formula was the prevailing promise for blacks until after World War II. It was this promise that supported the color-caste system and was largely responsible for the schism that arose between the black "haves" and the black "have nots." Bridging the gap between the more educated, affluent blacks and the more oppressed black masses is one of the primary goals of the Black Revolution.

Interestingly, just as there was relative agreement regarding the black man's greater athletic ability over whites, there was also general consensus for rejecting any overt endorsement of white-influenced leadership or of white criteria (items 5, 14, and 27). Last but not least, one has to point out the *fear* of the white man that is suggested here as a very significant factor in the behavior of blacks even until the early 40s. The responses to both items 28 and 34 indicate that considerable anxiety was associated with the possibility of increasing the white man's ire to any degree and that many of these black students were inclined to avoid doing so, even to the extent of hesitating to protest an illegal murder (such as a lynching) of a black person.

This has been a loose but, nevertheless, meaningful reexamination of one kind of data from one of several studies that attempted some objective assessment of the self-concept of American blacks in the 30s and early 40s. The interpretations drawn here are in general agreement with the findings of these studies as a whole.

From the Laboratory of Myself

In my efforts to study human behavior and to understand how persons function, my most important reference point as a psychologist, perhaps even my most useful laboratory, is myself—my own experiences, feelings, and reactions—the dangers of subjectivity notwithstanding. Is it not true that science must ultimately *make sense* to the scientist?

Edwards, in his chapter in this volume entitled "Looking Back on Growing up Black," makes the point that he was not spared the scarring experiences of black second-classness even though he did not grow up in an urban black ghetto. Every black person I have ever known in this country carries *some evidence*—and more often *a great deal of evidence*—of psychological scarring resulting from his growing-up experiences here, regardless of his particular background. It is well to remember that both the black bourgeoisie and the black masses from which they emerged have all been victims of the same racist society; there have merely been differences in experience (opportunity) and, therefore, in the defensive mechanisms developed for psychological survival. Failure to recognize this on the part of all factions of the black community is an unfortunate manifestation of a self-defeating involvement.

I grew up in a black urban ghetto. However, my family would be technically classified as black middle-class because my father was a physician. We too had our bad times during the depression, but we never seriously wanted for the basic necessities. We lived in the ghetto because my father insisted on the convenience and economy of having his residence and office under the same roof and in a location to suit his practice. Not comfortable with the black bourgeoisie, my father never engaged in that ostentatious and competitive society game. He had grown up under incredibly hard circumstances in Grove Hill, Alabama: his mother died when he was two; his father was an ex-slave, three-times owned before emancipation, and proud merely to be able to sign his own name.

One of my father's principal joys was supporting me in the pursuit of achievement. In growing up I led two lives: one in the sparsely integrated schools that he arranged for me to attend (for their educational advantages over ghetto schools), and the other as a relatively privileged child in the black community of an otherwise segregated town 56 miles above the Ohio River. I received a great deal of attention both at school and in the black community because I competed well academically with white students, something not generally expected of a "colored child." My ego was unduly inflated by this until I went to Fisk (a black college in Nashville, Tennessee) and learned—for my own good—that competing well with whites at home did not make me the smartest "colored child" in the world.

Here are four recollections illustrative of my personal involvement with adaptive inferiority.

Adaptive Inferiority and Its Resolution: Autobiographical Recollections

The first recollection, circa the late 1920s. This recollection begins with lines from the Song of Solomon (I: 5, 6).

> I am black, but comely,
>   O daughters of Jerusalem,
> Like the tents of Kedar,
>   Like the curtains of Solomon.
> Do not gaze at me because I am swarthy,
>   Because the sun has scorched me.
> My mother's sons were angry with me,
>   They made me keeper of the vineyards;
> But, my own vineyard I have not kept!

When I was a child in Sunday School (I grew up in the African Methodist Episcopal Church), we would be called on to read a verse from the *Bible*, and at times someone in a mischievous mood would read this passage from the Song of Solomon. Invariably there would be giggles and snickering. Sometimes the reading had a pointed meaning for a fumbling teacher who was not too well-liked and who may have been very dark besides. Her black students would take hostile delight in her embarrassment. But whether or not this was the case, these lines would always generate awkward amusement in the class. When the reading was finished, the teacher without further comment would call on the next child while the giggles subsided. The words *black* and *swarthy* in those days had self-reference implications that we could handle only in jest or in anger, or a combination of both; and the concept of their being related to comeliness or beauty was absurd! Black was *not* beautiful, and neither were we.

The second recollection, circa 1935–1936. There were 11 black students in my high school class of 381. I was one of the few black students who felt confident enough to have lunch in the high school cafeteria, even though the cafeteria was not segregated. All public facilities in the town, even lunch counters, were segregated; therefore, it took some anxiety-filled effort not to behave according to a pattern of segregation when in school. For some time I ate alone, but one day I was heartened when I was invited to join a regular table with seven of my white classmates, and the eight of us shared this table until we graduated. All of us were very much achievement motivated, most of our talk centered around assignments and other intellectual interests, and we found it mutually very beneficial. But there were moments of uneasiness for me in this group, especially on those rare occasions when someone cracked a joke with racial overtones or whenever a current downtown movie came into the conversation—a frequent occurrence. Because blacks were not allowed inside the downtown theaters, I could never discuss the movies. Incredibly, my classmates seemed unaware of the fact that I was barred from the theaters, and *I was ashamed to tell them*. I was ashamed to confront them with the fact that white society barred me from the downtown theaters because I felt that it was *a reflection on me*. It never occurred to me *then* that, if anything, it was a reflection on them.

The third recollection, circa 1961. It was 25 years later and just two years before the Black Revolution would take definite form. Our twenty-fifth high school class reunion was one of the most enjoyable experiences of my life. Devotion to school and class ran high among most of us (about 150 whites and 3 blacks returned for this event). It also was the time in 1961 when there was much excitement about the controversial "freedom rides" into the South in support of civil rights. In the midst of all the hilarity I found myself in a little group collected around one of our former teachers (all of whom had been white). She turned toward me and in patronizing tones of praise said, "Now take Roderick there. I *know he* wouldn't be a freedom rider, because if you have *something to offer,* you *don't need* to be a freedom rider."

I was taken off guard by this. Times had changed. But restraining myself in order not to spoil an otherwise great evening, I replied simply but firmly: "Did it ever occur to you that if I hadn't had the chance to attend this high school, I might not have as much to offer?" An awkward silence followed, and my old teacher and classmates learned in an effective one-shot trial that in 25 years times had changed and I had changed too. I could see that some of them, particularly the teacher, were shocked and disillusioned. It was an uneasy thought that this woman and many like her had helped to mold me; but it is relieving to recognize that by then my relationship to her and my classmates was no longer constrained by adaptive inferiority.

The fourth recollection, circa 1965–1966. It was during the very busy early days of the Black Revolution. A group of concerned black professionals organized a day-long workshop for the purpose of launching a systematic effort devoted to, among other things, bridging the understanding, communication, and cooperation gap between the "haves" and the "have nots" in Chicago's black community. This was a novel and timely development. The turnout was large, and the crowd exuded a mixture of enthusiasm and uncertainty about the success of the effort. There was an impressive array of keynote speakers including Lerone Bennett and Charles Hamilton.* Someone got up, reviewed the program for the day, and threw out a provocative challenge in words similar to these:

> Brothers and sisters, this is going to be a crucial day in our lives because we have gathered here for the purpose of coming to grips with ourselves, embracing our true identity, and closing ranks as a people. Most of you sitting out there have come here this morning thinking of yourselves as Negro. By the end of this day you must leave here thinking of yourselves as *black!*

To most of us this was indeed an uneasy challenge. We were told to make a psychological reversal, to embrace the concept of blackness that had for all our history and for all our lives been associated with so much anxiety. But since we had come to reshape our identity and to reclaim ourselves, we knew intuitively that ridding blackness of its anxiety was basic to the psychology of our self-reclamation. The day wore on with small groups in painful discussions —struggles, confessions about blackness, the experience of blackness, and the anxiety of blackness. But by the end of that day most of us had gone far toward a new acceptance of blackness freed from its anxiety. From that day on I accepted black as the identity for myself and my people.

The Black Revolution and Black-White Relations

Relationships between people achieve a mutuality and balance based on roles and role expectations. In stable relationships, roles and role expectations tend to support and reinforce each other. If one person begins to change his role and the concept he has of himself in that relationship, this disturbs the mutuality and balance

---

*For perhaps the best-known publication of each, see Bennett (1962) and Carmichael & Hamilton (1967) in References.

that the relationship had achieved in the past. Therefore, if the relationship is to maintain a mutuality and balance, a role change on the part of one party forces an accommodating role change on the part of the other. Put another way, in a continuing relationship the self-concept of one party will be affected by changes in the self-concept of the other party. During times when changes and accommodations to changes in role and self-concept are being worked through by the parties of a relationship, anxiety and friction within the relationship may be significantly heightened.

Whites in this country have related to blacks from a role of *assumed superiority,* and blacks have related to whites from a role of *adaptive inferiority.* That is, adaptive inferiority in blacks is seen to be not only reactive to assumed superiority in whites, but it has served to support and to perpetuate it. Assumed superiority and adaptive inferiority have been mutually supporting and perpetuating. The point is that the self-concept of whites to some degree has been organized around how they have perceived themselves in relation to blacks. It then seems reasonable to hypothesize that two self-concept processes are related to the Black Revolution. The first, as stated earlier, is central to it, and the second is a by-product of it: (1) there is a reintegration of self-concept on the part of blacks that entails the assumption of a positive sense-of-self and a rejection of adaptive inferiority vis-à-vis whites; and (2) there is a forced reintegration of self-concept on the part of whites that undermines their assumed superiority and promotes a more appropriate sense of self, especially vis-à-vis blacks. This forced reorganization of self-concept, which negates their assumed superiority, is threatening and anxiety-provoking to many whites and results in various kinds of resistance and "backlash" reactions against the change.

Fortuitous Influences on Black-White Relationships

There were two fortuitous influences from the world wars that had far-reaching effects on black-white relationships in this country. One had to do with experiences outside this country afforded two generations of black males (and quite a few females) during the wars and the subsequent armed involvements around the world. To experience something is to change; once the experience is realized, things are never quite the same. So it was with blacks relating to whites on the European continent, especially during and after the Second World War.

With European continentals, for the first time in my life I felt genuinely related to and accepted as another human being by whites. This was an uncanny experience that I did not trust at first. After all, so many of my growing up years had entailed relationships—"friendships"—with whites that began and ended at a school door. The reservations had been there in so many ways, from the tentative handshake to the geographical limitations placed on our association. Sometimes I felt almost like an untouchable! But it was different with the Europeans. There were no automatic barriers to rapport, and responses were free from anxiety. An invitation to family dinner was spontaneous and sincere. This had never happened to me in the United States.

Another unique experience was to find myself accepted by white people who were strongly prejudiced toward others. During the many weeks after the war that my outfit (all black) was stationed in a small German village, I was practically adopted by a German family and spent some time in their home daily. Frau Geiger was concerned when I did not seem well or a button was missing from my shirt. She was also concerned to tears when she and her husband were forced to billet three newly arrived white officers and she *thought perhaps* one was a *Jew*. I was flabbergasted to have a white woman crying on *my* shoulder because she so despised Jews. Until then, blacks had seemed to be the only truly rejected people in the world. Intellectually I knew better; but here, suddenly, I achieved a gut-level realization that this was not so, and it was difficult to integrate. During the process I felt I learned a great deal about racial prejudice.

These were the kinds of experiences that destroyed the aura of close personal relationships with whites. Whites were at last no more than ordinary human beings, and the assumed superiority of American whites was revealed for what it truly was in all its guises. Things back home could never be the same. And they were not.

In addition to American blacks learning something new about themselves and about whites while abroad, the other fortuitous influence on black-white relations in the United States from the wars was the rising importance of blacks for the country's position in international politics. The United States and the U. S. S. R. had emerged from World War II as arch-competitors. There was a new anti-colonial and nationalistic zeal throughout the African continent and among all colonized peoples that posed a threat to maintaining a favorable balance of power against communism. The rest of the world had a "show me" attitude toward this country's new position of world leadership and its old lip service to "all men are created equal."

Suddenly the liberal movement was on and the integration game was "in." It seemed sudden to me because it had taken public form during the years I had been overseas, from early 1944 to mid-1946. On my return, there it was in full bloom: Advertisements in streetcars promoted brotherhood. Radio programs debunked racial prejudice. Fashionable white liberals had at least one black guest at cocktail parties and other social gatherings. Heartening as all this was on the one hand, its suddenness and deliberateness—so uncharacteristic—led me to sense on the other hand that the underlying motivations were more internationally political than humanitarian, and we know that political winds do not always blow in the same direction. Regardless of the motivations, this public concern about racial relations conveyed to American blacks a change in their importance nationally and internationally. It was a local experience, derived from the war, which helped significantly to neutralize the adaptive inferiority of American blacks.

The Sham Is Dead!

The Black Revolution has resulted in the first genuine dialogue between blacks and whites in the history of this country. During three centuries of oppression, blacks surrendered their own true voice for the sake of survival. They lived in fear and functioned by means of defensive identification with the aggressor and adaptive inferiority. While this state of affairs prevailed no genuine dialogue was possible, for neither whites nor blacks could face the truth of themselves as human beings in relation to one another. Their relationship was a sham. Now the sham is dead, and this is the first complete accomplishment of the Black Revolution. Whatever the relationship is now between blacks and whites in this country, at least it is real. The cause is engaged.

The voice of alarm had been raised over the growing popularity of separatist sentiments in the national black community. Polarizations must be minimized, it is said, in support of the democratic ideals on which this country was founded. Could it be that polarizations initiated by blacks are more threatening than those initiated by whites? Regardless, a people cannot make its best contribution to life or to a democracy without a sure identity and a sound sense of self-esteem and integrity. For some blacks, a withdrawal "to the mountain" to contemplate fully one's sources and beginnings may be the surest way to self-reclamation. It is very necessary to find oneself in order to appreciate and defend this need on the part of others. Has this been the failing?

References

Bennett, L., Jr. *Before the Mayflower: A history of the Negro in America 1619–1962*. Chicago: Johnson, 1962.
Carmichael, S., & Hamilton, C. V. *Black power. The politics of liberation in America*. New York: Vintage Books, 1967.
Chrisman, R. The formation of a revolutionary black culture. *The Black Scholar*, 1970, **1**, 2–9.
Crowley, M. R. Cincinnati's experiment in Negro education: A comparative study of the segregated and mixed school. *Journal of Negro Education*, 1932, **1**, 25–33.
Davis, T. E. Some racial attitudes of Negro college and grade school students. *Journal of Negro Education*, 1937, **6**, 157–165.
A day to remember—more on the Washington march. *The Crisis*, 1963, **70** (8, Whole No. 606), 466–467.
Frazier, E. F. *Negro youth at the crossways: Their personality development in the middle states*. Washington, D. C.: The American Council on Education, 1940.
Gandy, J. M. A study of racial attitudes of Negro college students. Unpublished master's thesis, The Ohio State University, 1938.
Gregg, H. D. Non-academic and academic interests of Negro high school students in mixed and separate schools. *Journal of Negro Education*, 1938, 7, 41–47.
Grier, W. H., & Cobbs, P. M. *Black rage*. New York: Basic Books, 1968.
Hare, N. Wherever we are. *The Black Scholar*, 1971, **2**, 34–37.
Katz, W. L. *Eyewitness: The Negro in American history*. New York: Pitman, 1967.
Kerner, Otto (Chairman). *Report of the national advisory commision on civil disorders*. New York: Bantam Books, 1968.
Latimer, B. D. For William Edward Burghardt DuBois on his eightieth birthday. In L. Hughes and A. Bontemps (Eds.), *The Poetry of the Negro, 1746–1949*. Garden City, N. Y.: Doubleday, 1949. Pp. 208–209.
Morris, W. (Ed.) *The American heritage dictionary of the English language*. New York: Houghton Mifflin, 1969.
Pugh, R. W. A comparative study of the adjustment of Negro students in mixed and separate high schools. Unpublished master's thesis, The Ohio State University, 1941.
Pugh, R. W. A comparative study of the adjustment of Negro students in mixed and separate high schools. *Journal of Negro Education*, 1943, Fall Number, 607–616.
Pugh, R. W. Review of W. H. Grier & P. M. Cobbs, *Black rage*. *Contemporary Psychology*, 1969, **14**, 296–297.
Rogers, C. R. *On becoming a person*. Boston: Houghton Mifflin, 1961.

Chapter Two
Black Student Activism

The black student movement is not only an expression of the Black Revolution but a particular expression of international student unrest. It has its unique characteristics as a student movement, and it may prove to be the most vital effort within the Black Revolution. This latter conclusion is supported by the fact that the movement is a training ground for creative black leaders and activists, and it is continually influencing changes in higher education for both black and white.

The 1960s will be characterized historically as the decade of civil rights activism in the United States as well as the decade of international student unrest. As late as 1968, Mayhew (1968) made the observation, generally shared at the time, that the causes of student discontent were often difficult to understand. Student concerns were not consistent from one part of the world to the other, and the goals of student action seemed more often implicit than otherwise. Rossman (1968) and Keniston (Hall and Keniston, 1968) tended to feel that the young were beset with anxiety that was reactive to change and impermanence, to the contradiction between values stated and values lived, and to the increasing difficulty of finding meaning and identity in the context of today's social realities. To many of the young, the conflicts of war and peace, affluence and want, and black and white seemed needlessly ever-present.

With the passing of time the concerns that are central to

student activism have become more clearly articulated. Conant (1971) offers the following summary of them:

> ... that the wealth of the nation be brought to bear on social and environmental problems, as a matter of priority over luxury consumption, profiteering, and war; ... that our political ingenuity be applied to reducing international tensions, as a matter of priority over power relationships, economic exploitation, and ideological competition ... [and that] participatory democracy [gain ascendency] over institutionalized authoritarianism [p. 15].

He further specifies "racial integration, ecological and environmental problems, new arrangements in federal-local relations, the elimination of economic poverty, population control, United States leadership in world affairs, disarmament, and the Bomb [p. 20]" as the likely political issues of the 1970s, and he predicts that continued unrest and protest action among students will be governed by how effectively these issues are engaged.

All of the issues above are concerns of both black and white student activists. Black activists, however, have one overriding concern—that is, the realization of the Black Revolution and black liberation. Other issues take priority to the extent that they seem directly related to achieving these. Therefore, black student activism has a consistent national focus, clearly defined. This is not the case with white student activism, where the focus can vary from day to day and from place to place and issues may not always be clear and specific.

Civil rights was the principal focal issue in this country that gave rise to both black and white student activism in the 60s. In February 1960, black students initiated the lunch counter sit-ins in Greensboro, North Carolina, as a protest over segregated public facilities (see Table 1–1). White students in the North sympathetically supported the sit-ins through boycotts of national chain stores. By May 1961, white and black students were collaborating in integrated freedom rides into the Deep South. Soon the Student Nonviolent Coordinating Committee (SNCC) was born as an integrated student-activist organization, and it remained so until about 1966 (Stanford, 1971). By that time the growth of the black consciousness-concept and the necessity for black self-reclamation demanded a closing of ranks and the exclusion of whites for the purpose of consolidating the black community and promoting reliance on black leadership. SNCC became black, and the black and white student-activist movements became polarized. This dispensed with any blurring of the focus and goals of the black student movement.

Blacks constitute 11.2 percent of the U. S. population. Between 1965 and 1970 the number of blacks 18 to 24 years of age enrolled in college nearly doubled. Now one of every six blacks in that age group is enrolled in college (compared with one of every three whites —*Chicago Tribune,* 1971). It is likely that an increasing proportion of blacks will find their way to college; therefore, the ranks of black student activists are likely to grow. This is not to suggest that every black student is or will become actively involved in the movement, for the best evidence is that only a minority of students are activists (Bay, 1967). The more students there are, however, the greater the probability for larger numbers of activists. Further, even in the absence of hard statistics, there is every indication that the overwhelming majority of black students is caught up in "black consciousness" and is strongly supportive of the movement, whether actively involved or not.

Perhaps at this point there should be some clarification of the categories of involvement in the student movement that are used here. Four levels of involvement are proposed: (1) disengaged, (2) aware-sympathetic, (3) activist, and (4) radical. The best guess is that the great majority of black students would be covered by the second and third categories, with the second category being considerably the largest of the four. Another *probable* distinction between black and white student groups is that the activist category constitutes a larger percentage among black students than among white and that a far larger percentage of black students are "aware-sympathetic" vis-á-vis their movement than are white students vis-á-vis theirs. These assumptions are in part suggested by Laskin's (1971) survey of the literature. Further, it can be assumed that the line of demarcation between the aware-sympathetic and the activist categories for black students is rather fluid and is responsive to the urgency of particular local and national developments.

The black student activist is one who assumes the role of active change agent in the cause of the Black Revolution and black liberation and devotes significant amounts of his time and effort in organized activities supportive of the movement both on and off the campus. He is politicized and by and large works and hopes for change through measures short of violent revolution. The black student activist is not necessarily nonviolent, but he is not a radicalized, violent revolutionary.

The disengaged category of black students is probably the second largest category of the four. This category would comprise those students who are disinterested, "out of it," or in some instances even unsympathetic to the movement.

Radicalized revolutionaries are still a very small minority among black college students (as they are among whites); however, as among whites, there are indications that their numbers are slowly but steadily growing. The extent to which the number of radicals increases may be related to the amount of hardened resistance the activists meet in their efforts to bring about systematic change. As Conant (1971) has pointed out:

> The radicalization of the SDS during the 1960's is a dramatic example of youthful dedication to constructive change that became discouraged and disillusioned in one encounter after another over government policies of military victory in Southeast Asia, gradualism in minority civil rights, opportunism in poverty programs, and law-and-order over justice in response to protest [p. 17].

In summary, it is hypothesized that on the basis of proportions of the black student population, the four categories would rank as follows from largest to smallest: (1) aware-sympathetic, (2) disengaged, (3) activist, and (4) radical. And the aware-sympathetic and activist categories combined would constitute a sizable majority of black students. This is admittedly an educated guess that would be interesting to investigate.

Black student activism has another uniqueness because it operates in two distinct settings of higher learning—the black and the integrated. Differences between these settings influence the nature of secondary concerns. But interestingly, the primary concern in the immediate academic situation is the same whether integrated or black —that is, students want the educational experience to be "relevant" and meaningful to them as black people, and to support in every sense the development of black esteem.

In the integrated institution this concern is expressed by demands for increased black student enrollment, black faculty, and black studies courses that focus on black achievements, the black experience, and solutions for the black condition in this country. Black consciousness in integrated institutions is expressed by preference for separation in living arrangements, extracurricular programs, and social activities. In situations where black and white come together, the spirit is to compete well and to cooperate as equals. In things political pertaining to black students, the black activists are generally well in command. Their most troublesome problems are organizational inexperience and working constructively with the few generally vocal, aggressive, and intellectually bright advocates of the radical position. Whether the institution is integrated or black, one of its most valuable educational advantages is the setting it provides to test methods and strategies for coping with problems of living in a complex society. The integrated campus provides a particular opportunity for developing ways of securing one's position as a black person on a day-to-day basis in a predominately white society. Black students in an integrated setting take for granted that the institution is basically white in its orientation and purposes. Their goals are to establish a consideration for blacks as a people and a relationship with the academic community following a model that might be equally appropriate later in the overall society. For example, the formal petition to the administration by the organized black students at Northwestern University on April 22, 1968, began with the following preamble and first demand:

> We, the black students at Northwestern University, have found the academic, cultural, and social conditions for us on campus deplorably limited. In order to counteract the physical, emotional, and spiritual strains we have been subjugated to, in order to find some meaning and purpose in our being here, we demand that the following conditions be immediately met.
> We demand, firstly, that a policy statement be issued from the administration deploring the viciousness of "white racism" and insuring that all conscious or unconscious racist policies, practices, and institutions existing now on campus will no longer be tolerated ["Documents," 1968].

The challenge to black activism in the nonintegrated institution of higher learning is that the nominally black institution become *authentically black* in its orientation and purposes. The aims of the black student movement on the black college campus are more far-reaching and often more difficult to achieve than on an integrated campus. The background is somewhat as follows.

Being white, being black, and becoming liberally educated are not inherently related. Because of the black man's history in this country, however, significant relationship between one's being black and the educational process has been forced. This is so because a *liberal education is rightfully directed toward the development of the total person.* Since the conventional educational experience in this country is a product of white culture, it quite naturally supports the white student in his consolidation of identity, self-acceptance, and self-esteem. In the main, every experience that a white student has in college affirms his worthwhileness not only as a person but as a *white* person. In significant ways this has not been the case for the black student. In most black educational institutions of higher learning, especially the more traditional ones, there have been and still are aspects of the educational experience that tend to negate the student's developing an appropriate identity and self-acceptance. This results from the peculiar history of these institutions.

Not only were white institutions of higher learning in this country founded by whites but most of the traditional black colleges and universities were founded by whites. In those days (latter nineteenth century) they were the "radical" whites. They set out to challenge the still widely held belief that black people on the whole were uneducable and incapable of integration into western culture. Blacks have profited from the fact that they took up this challenge; but unhappily, since these white educational missionaries took themselves as a model, there was for the black student the insidious implication that becoming educated and acculturated meant becoming as much like white as possible, even to the point of rejecting black physical characteristics, especially skin color and type of hair. As a result, educated and upward-mobile blacks, with the encouragement of the overall white society, became significantly caught up in the color-caste business. At some of the traditional black colleges there was a time when sororities could be distinguished by differences in the average skin color of their members. Such things were privately acknowledged, but they never emerged as public issues. It was unheard of that a student, faculty member, or administrator had the conviction and the courage to question such practices openly. They were passively accepted or supported overtly or covertly with an attitude of inevitability.

The same practices existed on integrated campuses as well, but their impact was diluted because of the relatively small numbers of blacks and the fact that the integrated campus did not usually impose a closed social system on its black students as was the case in the majority of black colleges and universities. A larger number of black students at integrated colleges was more likely to live off campus and to have a social life in the black community. The closed social system that characterized the average black college campus served to sharpen the impact of a color-caste system to the extent that it existed, especially when it involved black faculty and administration as well as students. In those times, however, courage to react was not forthcoming because anxiety was too much conditioned to blackness, and the position of blacks as a whole in the country was so oppressive that the most accepted position was that each individual had to work out his own best solution. This was essentially the situation until after World War II. As I pointed out earlier, the be-like-white success formula has now been revealed as a fraud, an empty promise, and psychological sabotage; but its residuals are slow to fade.

There is another factor, very much a part of the circumstance of all but a few black colleges and universities, that generates a difficult psychological dilemma for black activism and its basic goals —the promotion of black self-esteem and black liberation. The great majority of black colleges and universities are either state supported or privately endowed. This means that their existence depends on funds coming either through the state's white power structure or from white philanthropy. A sense of completeness as a person, however, requires a rejection of controlling dependency relationships and the development of appropriate autonomy and mastery over one's welfare and destiny. How much your own man can you ever be as long as you are *basically dependent on and controlled by another*? There is not one black institution of higher learning in this country whose continued existence could be guaranteed by its own alumni. The few black institutions of higher learning that are supported almost entirely by blacks are church related; but they tend to be the very poorest in facilities and faculty. Thus black institutions are still dependent on white money or the white power structure for their continued existence. This is a fact that takes the sting out of black activism on many black campuses, and the solution to this dilemma seems far off.

Black student activists generally eschew the theoretical and abstract and focus on what can be practically applied to a situation for the quickest possible results. For example, members of the Black Student Psychological Association have criticized the field of psychology for being too "theoretically oriented" and having failed to utilize psychological knowledge for "action-oriented real-world-based problem-solving programs" to alleviate the plight of the oppressed. The following points have been stated (Black Student Psychological Association, 1970):

    a. Psychology as a science and a profession must become more functional and useful to the black community. The concern is what can psychology do now—not what are the current theoretical and research issues.
    b. More blacks must become trained psychologists so that these goals may be more readily achieved.
    c. Testing and research which yield results with consistently negative implications for blacks as a group are to be disregarded because of evidently invalid criteria. This position applies to college entrance examinations as well.

The following is my attempt to summarize the overall goals of black student activism as they have evolved to date.

Goals Applicable to Both Black and Integrated Campuses:

1. The pursuit of the authentic life for black people through the promotion of the Black Revolution and black liberation.
2. Higher education must be made more relevant to social realities, and specifically to problems of black people. Black students must actively participate in the progressive reform of the purposes and methods of higher education and in the reorientation of its values toward the human and away from the material.
3. Higher education must be rid of every vestige of white racism, and no aspect of the educational experience must overtly or covertly serve to undermine the self-esteem of black students.
4. Education must be used for developing oneself into an effective social change agent, and every campus must be seen as a setting for testing methods and strategies for promoting the welfare of black people.
5. The numbers of blacks receiving a higher education must be increased.
6. Anxiety related to competing intellectually with whites must be resolved.
7. The national black community must be con-

solidated. The black middle class must be reoriented toward the enhancement of relations between the black haves and have nots. Care must be taken that acquiring a higher education does not generate a schism between the educated and the less educated black masses.
8. International communication and cooperation between blacks must be encouraged and maintained.

Goals More Specific to the Black Campus:

9. The college or university must serve as a community center for blacks, providing free facilities for community programs and encouraging community participation in the life of the institution at every possible level.
10. Education on the black campus must emphasize the development of political awareness and it must give training in the nature of political activism and effectiveness.
11. A goal specific to the radical position is that "the black college student must make the black college a base for revolutionary black nationalist thought [Stanford, 1971, p. 30]."
12. Means must be devised for insuring that the survival of black institutions of higher learning is not solely dependent on white philanthropy or funds controlled by the white power structure.

Everyone is aware of the fact that something happened to student activism in the fall of 1970. Conant (1971) calls it "the new ambivalence," reactive to "... the deep frustration and despair of youth who were frightened by Kent State ... [p. 22]." Laskin (1971) refers to a retrenchment since Kent State (May 4, 1970) and refers to an interpretation by Eva Jefferson (the former black President of Northwestern's student body) that students are now turning to challenges "that are at least humanly possible [p. 12]." He makes clear, however, that her position still revolves around "... a guiding light of radical change and this is expounded upon whenever the chance arises [p. 12]." It is an interesting commentary on our society, and even on student activism, that the Jackson State incident of May 14, 1970, in which two black students were killed and eleven injured by police action on a black college campus, did not cause the shock nor the reaction that followed Kent State; for example, authors such as

Conant and Laskin, in assessing influences on subsequent student activism, give it no mention.

Those who are involved as faculty and administrators in higher education today cannot escape the impact of live, searching, probing human beings. Rationalizations, abstractions, and "administrative processes" offer no refuge. The sham is dead! That this is true is a healthy development, for it promotes the viable education that offers hope in the face of the proliferation of social problems and threats to mankind's survival.

Direct participation in the higher education of black students is no doubt especially challenging and even stressful at times to the white person, particularly if he or she is a part of the faculty or administration of a black institution. Anyone—black or white—who would participate constructively in the education of the black student must have gone far in the search for himself, because the black student today is *in search of himself* and not merely in search of an "educational opportunity," as was the case in former years. Ultimately, no gratification exceeds that which comes from the search for oneself and the realization of having participated in, and perhaps facilitated, this search on the part of another.

References

Bay, C. Political and apolitical students: Facts in search of a theory. *Journal of Social Issues*, 1967, **23**, 76–91.

Black Student Psychological Association (BSPA), University of Michigan. Unpublished report of the Committee on Faculty Recruitment, 1970.

Chicago Tribune, editorial, July 28, 1971, p. 12.

Conant, R. W. The prospects for revolution. *The University of Chicago Magazine*, 1971, **63**, 13–23.

Documents. Black and white at Northwestern. *Integrated Education*, 1968, **6**, 33–48.

Hall, M. H., & Keniston, K. A conversation with Kenneth Keniston, or the psychology of student activists. *Psychology Today*, 1968, **2**, 16*ff*.

Laskin, J. Who is the student activist? Unpublished paper, Loyola University of Chicago, 1971.

Mayhew, L. B. Changing the balance of power. *Saturday Review*, August 17, 1968, 48*ff*.

Rossman, M. The two faces of youth. Review of K. Keniston, *Young radicals: Notes on committed youth*. *Saturday Review*, August 17, 1968, 50–51.

Stanford, Max. Black Nationalism and the Afro-American student. *The Black Scholar*, 1971, **2**, 27–31.

Part Two

Black Psychologists at Work

Chapter Three
Psychotherapy under Varying Conditions of Race*

LaMaurice H. Gardner

The collection of writings in this volume on the personal and professional experiences of black psychologists provides an important opportunity to bring more balance into existing literature on such topics as "the black experience," "the black personality," and the dynamics of the intra- and interracial relationship patterns of blacks. It is a most unfortunate and perhaps telling situation that so much of what has been published on these and related topics contains so little that can be described as acceptable scientific findings. Too much of what has been written contains evidence of distortion and misunderstanding based on a failure by research investigators to control more or less subtle ethnocentric "racial experimenter effects [Sattler, 1970]." As blacks have become increasingly familiar with the contents of this literature on race, they have recoiled from its misrepresentations and its potential for reinforcing the negative racial stereotypes that continue to divide our nation. It is for this reason that many blacks have called for a moratorium on all further efforts by white investigators to study, test, and explain the psychological and social characteristics of blacks.

A close examination of psychiatric and psychological literature on race clearly indicates that investigators have largely failed to

---

*This chapter, an original contribution to the 1970 Loyola University of Chicago Symposium by Black Psychologists, has also been published in *Psychotherapy: Theory, Research and Practice*, 1971, **8**, 78–87. It is reprinted here with permission.

appreciate the methodological complexities involved in psychosocial research under interracial conditions. Although early research in the physical sciences demonstrated the need to control "the human equation" in the collection of scientific data, only in recent years have behavioral scientists begun to concentrate research efforts on the effects of experimenter and subject bias and expectancy on results obtained in otherwise well-designed studies (Rosenthal, 1966). The results of these investigations demonstrate that experimenter variables may—and often do—influence such dimensions of research as data collection, hypothesis testing, and the interpretation of results.

In a recent paper on "Racial 'Experimenter Effects' in Experimentation, Testing, Interviewing and Psychotherapy," Sattler (1970) made the following observations:

> The studies show that subjects are influenced by the experimenter's race. However the extent and direction of the influence depends on many factors including (a) the task content, (b) instructional set, (c) reinforcement conditions, (d) geographical location of study, (e) subject variables such as age, race, family background, socioeconomic level, and attitudes, (f) experimenter variables such as race of experimenter team, attitudes, residence, and socioeconomic level, and (g) dependent measures [p. 155].

Sattler's paper presents an excellent overview of issues and findings in inter- and intraracial behavioral research. But as he points out, the literature on the effects of race on therapist-client interaction in psychotherapy is weak and fairly one-sided. Few controlled investigations have been attempted in this area of study. Although several articles have attempted to detail the parameters of white-therapist/black-client interaction, few exist on the subjects of black-therapist/white-client or black-therapist/black-client relationships. This paper attempts a more detailed examination of therapist-client relationships in psychotherapy under varying conditions of race, with an emphasis on ways both therapist and client expectancy and bias contribute to the clinical phenomena on which writers have based their contributions to the psychology of race.

White Therapist/Black Client: Therapist Variables

Because of the nature and orientation of our society, its members are characterized by an almost universal tendency to develop unconscious racial bigotry (Rosen & Frank, 1962). Recognizing this, a number of writers have noted the need for white and black psychotherapists to come to terms with their feelings about race before attempting to treat members of minority groups (Adams, 1950; Curry, 1964a; Grier & Cobbs, 1968; Heine, 1950; Rosen & Frank, 1962; and so on). A large portion of the frequently cited literature on the personality structure and interaction patterns of blacks has issued from observations made by therapists in the course of intensive psychoanalytically oriented therapeutic relationships. It is to this literature that therapists—black and white—frequently turn when preparing to work with and understand their black clients. Too often this literature is digested uncritically and with little realization that paper never refused ink. Thus when the therapist approaches his black client, he may do so harboring assumptions, mental sets, and beliefs of questionable validity gathered from the professional literature, from the attitudes and pronouncements of his training supervisors, and from his own conscious and unconscious attitudes about blacks.

Psychoanalytic training, through the didactic analysis and control work, attempts to examine those conscious and unconscious attitudes and dispositions in the candidate that may impair his ability to understand objectively and to establish empathic rapport with clients. However, there is no indication anywhere in psychoanalytic literature that training analysts give adequate attention to the analysis of unconscious antiblack prejudice in white candidates. This may well account for the patronizing and paternalistic attitudes that so frequently characterize psychoanalytic papers on the "Negro personality."

Although psychoanalytic writers have made important contributions to our understanding of the interaction between native endowment and psychosocial experience in the shaping of individual personality, their contributions to the understanding of personality development and adaptation in blacks contain a curious admixture of objective reporting, ethnocentric distortion, updated racial mythology, paternalistic exhortation, and poppycock. Thomas (1962) has noted that cultural stereotypes regarding the inferiority of American blacks appear frequently in psychiatric and psychoanalytic literature. But instead of offering genetic-constitutional explanations for this supposed inferiority as was true of the earlier literature (for example, see Klineberg, 1944), the current trend is to account for it in dynamic-experiential terms based on the well-documented oppression and discrimination blacks experience.

A frequently cited study by Kardiner and Ovesey (1951) provides a good example of this trend. Based on the psychoanalytic and psychodiagnostic investigation of 25 black clients, Kardiner and Ovesey described the following characteristics as being fairly prominent in the personality organization of blacks:

1. Superficiality
2. Apathy and resignation
3. Repressed hostility
4. The wish to be white
5. Identification with feces
6. Intragroup aggression
7. White ego-ideal
8. Inclined to gamble
9. Magical thinking
10. Inclined to alcoholism
11. Unconsciously resentful & antisocial
12. Weak superego development
13. Disorderly, unsystematic
14. Sexual freedom
15. Reject education
16. Poor discipline in childhood
17. Maternal neglect & rejection
18. Little respect for parents
19. Psychologically crippled
20. Distrustful
21. Live for the moment
22. Hedonistic

These formulations are intended to describe a model personality pattern in terms of which the entire black group is to be understood. Such an approach to the psychosocial study of groups is no less than methodological recklessness (Doob, 1965). Far less subtle examples of stereotypic thinking in white therapists are also found in the literature. In an early article, Lauretta Bender (1939) wrote that characteristic traits in black children such as laziness and the ability to dance are a reflection of specific brain-impulse tendencies. More recently some writers have had a tendency to suggest that the greatest psychological tragedy to befall the black man in the United States was his premature emancipation. Hunter and Babcock (1967) have proposed that with the emancipation proclamation "the psychologically immature Negro was given the choice of remaining within the symbiotic plantation-slave common membrane or of delivering himself into the world external to it. In view of his unprepared ego, the permission to individuate, given by law to the Negro slave in 1863, was essentially a useless privilege [pp. 160–161]." Wilson and Lantz (1957) also expressed the belief that the conditions of slavery were more favorable to the psychological security of blacks. They argued that the increasing incidence of mental illness and psychological uncertainty among blacks was directly associated with the movement of the group toward equality with whites.

These assertions are undocumented and hardly qualify as

scientific. They are paternalistic, ethnocentric, and no more rational than the following statements of a European psychiatrist studying the Tembu of Africa. He wrote:

> Although the scarcity of meat in the diet is no doubt conducive to stock theft, the native's general attitude towards food and his stomach is indicative of powerful oral needs, which reflect the infantile nature of his culture [Doob, 1965, p. 394].

Here the obvious association between poor diet and concern with the digestive apparatus is overlooked due to preformed attitudes about African culture and the mentality of its people. It is this specific tendency to impose unconscious racial stereotypes on the material produced by blacks that constitutes the greatest threat to real understanding and effective psychotherapeutic interaction in the white-therapist/black-client combination. The ways in which these attitudes influence diagnostic and treatment relationships with blacks are many. Hollingshead and Redlich (1958) have already demonstrated the tendency of white middle-class therapists to discriminate against members of minority groups and the poor. Additional documentation of this phenomenon is found in a study by Yamamoto, James, Bloombaum, and Hattem (1967) showing that blacks who seek mental health services in a clinic staffed by white professionals are less likely to receive dynamic individual or group psychotherapy, are seen for fewer sessions, and have higher attrition rates than white clients. These investigators found a significant positive relationship existing between therapist ethnocentricity and black attrition rates.

Recognizing the frequency with which conscious and unconscious racial bias influences the white therapist's perception of his black client, it is not surprising that they often report that black clients tend to be resentful and suspicious (Rosen & Frank, 1962), difficult to establish rapport with (St. Clair, 1951), untreatable or unreachable (Calnek, 1970), incapable of insight, and so on.

A disclaimer must be entered at this point. What is being said here should not be taken to imply that it is more desirable that black clients have black therapists. Not at all. My purpose here is only to highlight the extent to which unconscious racial attitudes *may* cause white therapists to misunderstand and misinterpret the behavior of blacks. Black therapists have their own problems keeping unconscious racial attitudes from influencing their work with black and white clients. We will deal with these later. Basically I agree with Heine (1950) that the only barrier to the effective treatment of black clients by white therapists is the therapist's own unresolved racial prejudice. White therapists who are more or less free of racial prejudice and who have achieved the skill and psychological integrity necessary for the conduct of psychotherapy may be as effective with black clients as with any client.

Let us turn now to some of the specific challenges and pitfalls common to the white-therapist/black-client situation.

The history of race relations in the United States has so sensitized us all that the initial phase of any interracial relationship between strangers is likely to be characterized by cautious attempts by each party to discern gross or subtle indications of the racial attitudes of the other. On the basis of what is perceived or fantasied, each person adjusts his behavior in such a way as to minimize vulnerability and maximize the ability to cope. When the therapist is white and the client black, due consideration must be given the complicating aspects of culturally conditioned interaction tendencies that will influence transference and countertransference phenomena but are actually independent of them (Curry, 1964a).

Where the white therapist is inclined to deal with personal conflict through defensive flight and avoidance, the black client who stirs up unconscious racial attitudes in him is likely to be rejected either through referral to another therapist or through the use of more impersonal treatment procedures such as drug therapy. On the other hand the therapist may resort to defensive denial, failing to recognize and deal not only with his own racial feelings but also with those of his black client.

Frequently observed in the relationship between white therapists and black clients is the therapists' tendency to ward off their own racial hostility and conflict by resorting to strong reaction formations. When this is the case, the therapist may manifest an inclination to be oversympathetic and overindulgent in an effort to conceal feelings of guilt about his racial attitudes (Adams, 1950), or he may overlook severe psychopathology in his black clients (Grier & Cobbs, 1968) and attribute the source of all their problems to cultural and racial conflict (Adams, 1950).

White Therapist/Black Client: Client Variables

The black client entering psychotherapy with a white therapist is likely to experience considerable anxiety about racial differences

(Kennedy, 1952). These anxieties may take such forms as fear, suspicion, verbal constriction, strained and unnatural reactions, feigning stupidity (Sattler, 1970), "acting white" (Calnek, 1970), ingratiation or open resentment (Rosen & Frank, 1962), and hostility (St. Clair, 1951). Regardless of the form his anxieties assume, the black client in the initial stages of psychotherapy with a white therapist will consciously and unconsciously subject him to a series of tests to determine the extent to which the client is accepted as an individual and is free to express feelings that might make him particularly vulnerable to rejection, insult, and humiliation. Because this is most often the case in the white-therapist/black-client relationship, the development of a working alliance (Greenson, 1967) may be delayed longer than would be the case in an intraracial situation. This delay has caused some therapists to believe that it is difficult to establish rapport and a workable therapeutic relationship with black clients (St. Clair, 1951).

The black client who fears alienating his white therapist by expressing resentment of the discrimination to which he as a black is subjected may actually repress and deny ever having suffered its malignant effects (Sattler, 1970). He may also demonstrate what Waite (1968) has called the "nigger complex," systematically avoiding any behavior that might be taken to exemplify the fabled attributes summarized in the stereotype of "the nigger." Such a client will have special difficulty expressing feelings and fantasies associated with the hostile transference (St. Clair, 1951) and may strongly repress oedipal material because of the taboo against sexual competition with the white male (Adams, 1950).

On the other hand, some black clients will react to the interracial therapeutic situation by overemphasizing their blackness and the patterns of discrimination to which they have been exposed. In this manner they may use their minority status (a) to conceal basic personality difficulties (Sommers, 1953), (b) to put the therapist on the defense, (c) to avoid personal involvement in the therapeutic task by substituting social problems for personal ones (Heine, 1950), or (d) to express through misplacement and acting-out a deeply entrenched hostility toward authority (St. Clair, 1951). Adams (1950) has noted that blacks characterized by oral demanding tendencies may spend considerable time in psychotherapy discussing racial problems, being happy to find discrimination where there is none and rather unhappy to find evidence that they are being treated fairly.

Each black client will deal with his interracial motives and anxieties in his own unique manner. And his ego will resort to the same coping and defensive patterns that characterize his efforts at conflict resolution in general. It is important that a therapist not lose sight of the individuality of his black client. A number of writers have erred, believing that in black clients individualized ego development is impeded by and is subordinate to the effects of traumatic experiences of the group. Writing from this perspective, Kennedy (1952) described black clients in general as indiscriminately hostile and expressed the belief that the primary source of neurosis in blacks is the long-standing frustration each experiences in relation to his wish to be white!

In his transactions with black clients, the white therapist must make every effort to eliminate bias and stereotype from his perception of the client. He must also examine the possible countertransference gratification he may derive from working with blacks. Countertransference motives in white therapists that frequently impede progress in the treatment of black clients include (a) the need for a power role, (b) the need for affection, (c) the need to enlarge the scope of social experiences, (d) the need to expiate racial guilt (Sattler, 1970), and (e) the need to seek vicarious gratification through the sexual and aggressive activities of their black clients.

Effective psychotherapy with black clients requires dealing with intense feelings about race and experiences of discrimination, but the white therapist must avoid the pitfall of attempting to treat the "black problem" and losing sight of the difficulties of his individual client (Heine, 1950). And if the white therapist is also a member of a minority group that has been the subject of discrimination, he must be careful to avoid the paternalism implied in suggesting that blacks should follow the examples of his own group if they are to be more successful in advancing the group's socioeconomic status. If the white therapist gets "hung-up" on issues of race exclusively, the therapy will have only limited effectiveness. It is the primary task of a therapist to encourage the development of a strong working alliance between himself and his client. He contributes to this "by his consistent emphasis on understanding and insight, by his continued analysis of the resistances, and by his compassionate, empathic, straightforward, and non-judgmental attitudes [Greenson, 1967]."

Black Therapist/White Client: Client Variables

Very little has been reported in the literature on the parameters and dynamics of psychotherapeutic interaction when the therapist is black and the client white. There are many reasons for this neglect, perhaps the most significant being that only in recent years have a significant number of blacks become professional psychotherapists. From the limited literature that exists on the experiences of black therapists in the treatment of white clients, it is clear that the color of the therapist plays an important role in determining the contents of the relationship. Curry (1964a) has noted that when the therapist is black, his skin color alone can elicit fantasies and symbolic processes in white clients that may have profound effects on the process of therapy. He suggests that in the treatment of white clients the black therapist will have to deal not only with standard resistance and transference phenomena but also with culturally conditioned resistances stimulated by the fact that he is black.

A number of writers (Curry, 1964a; Hamilton, 1966; Sterba, 1947; Rodgers, 1955) have pointed out the symbolic associations that cluster around the colors black and white in our western culture. White is most often associated with cleanliness, divinity, illumination, purity, goodness, awareness, life, knowledge, and heaven. Black is associated with the mysterious, the exotic, the savage, dirt, sin, badness, inferiority, darkness, sleep, death, emotional abandon, feces, man's fallen state, evil, ignorance, the unconscious, power, magic, libido, Hades, Judas, and Satan. Psychoanalysts dealing with the fantasies of white clients about blacks have noted the frequency with which such fantasies disclose an unconscious identification between the black—especially the black male—and the oedipal father (Sterba, 1947; Rodgers, 1955), the unwanted sibling (Sterba, 1947), the phallic-sadistic rapist (Rodgers, 1955), and the indulging, uncritical mammy (Grier, 1967). These observations can be documented in the associations, fantasies, and dreams produced by white clients in treatment with black therapists. However, it is important to note that these culturally conditioned preformed transference tendencies may, if properly handled and interpreted, act as a catalyst to the discovery and working through of deeply entrenched neurotic attitudes more rapidly than would be the case with a white therapist (Grier, 1967).

Not infrequently, a white client will prefer a black therapist because of certain past or present experiences with blacks or because of particular personality problems or dispositions. Young whites in the midst of antiestablishment rebellion may prefer a black therapist because of identification with the insults and oppression blacks have experienced from the system. This kind of identification was illustrated in an article that appeared in a popular magazine under the title "The

Student as Nigger." Others may feel more comfortable and secure in discussing their problems with blacks because they fear less the possibility of their secrets filtering back into the community through the indiscretions of the therapist. Some may seek out a black therapist because they are too ashamed to discuss certain topics with white therapists. An example of this is the white female client who has engaged in sexual activities with black men. In these cases the black therapist may be especially prone to experience difficulty in the handling of transference and countertransference phenomena. Overall, white clients under 40 years of age have less difficulty accepting black therapists than their older counterparts.

The specific ways in which white clients will relate to the blackness of their therapist prove consistently to follow reaction patterns typical of their modes of coping and defending in diverse areas of living. Oral-dependent clients may relate to the black therapist as an idealized maternal object who has limitless supplies of love and oral gratification to bestow. Narcissistic-seductive female clients may be inclined to see a black male therapist as unable to resist the amorous advances of a white woman and will directly or indirectly invite a sexual affair. Clients subject to secretiveness and shame will closely guard disclosing to family and peers that the therapist is black. Clients with problems of sibling rivalry will fantasize themselves not only as the black therapist's favorite client but as his only white client. In my own experiences, white female clients may react to the discovery that the black therapist has other white patients with jealousy, rage, and even conversion symptoms. On the other hand, white clients whose difficulties include tendencies to verbalize or act out hostile destructive impulses may attack the black therapist in racial terms. They may engage in extensive tirades against blacks—excluding the therapist, of course—or make direct or indirect remarks about the therapist's "uppity" status by accusing him of fantasizing himself a black Jesus or dubbing him "Booker T. Freud" (Curry, 1964b). With white male clients it is not at all unusual for the black therapist to find a reluctance to disclose material that might indicate oedipal competition. White male clients who have had sexual affairs with black females or who have visited black prostitutes seem characteristically to delay revealing these facts until late in the therapy. Often white male clients who have had no such experiences will, at the point when the oedipal transference becomes prominent, begin to express fantasies and desires of having affairs with black females. White female clients in the midst of the oedipal transference will demonstrate longings for and expectations of sexual gratification from the black male therapist.

It has been my experience that a prominent preoccupation of white clients who enter into psychotherapeutic relationships with black therapists is the fear that the therapist will detect in them conscious or unconscious racism. Because of this fear white clients may avoid the discussion of any association, fantasy, or dream that they believe might disclose the existence of negative racial attitudes. These clients may become enraged at the slightest suggestion of the therapist that their material discloses an attempt to express or avoid feelings they are experiencing that relate to the subject of race. This type of sensitivity was demonstrated by a white female client who actually gave little evidence of harboring racist attitudes. During a particular psychoanalytic session in which she discussed fascism and Hitler's extermination of Jews she repeatedly asked "am I not seeing something?" When the therapist translated this question into "Am I a Nazi or something?" it became clear that she feared that the therapist would interpret her discussion of facism as evidence of a hidden racist attitude.

In some instances white clients may abruptly refrain from voicing legitimate complaints about the conditions with which they are forced to cope. When questioned about this, they may express feelings of guilt, stating to the black therapist: "I really have no right to complain about my situation when you and your people have suffered so much more" (Curry, 1964b). The black therapist must expose this kind of oversolicitousness as resistance if a thorough examination of the client's difficulties is to continue.

Some white clients deal with the interracial aspects of the relationship by denying the blackness of the therapist. An example of this tendency is seen in a letter Curry (1964b) received from one of his white clients stating "the longer I worked with you the whiter you became." Such statements may be either positive or derogatory. They may indicate that, for the white client, the awareness of racial differences declined during the course of psychotherapy, or they may represent accusation that the black therapist has forgotten his roots and has adopted attitudes kindred to those common to the white bigot. A young white woman who entered analysis at the suggestion of her sister—who later joined the John Birch Society—had since late adolescence thoroughly repudiated the idea of obtaining social or sexual gratification within her own group and spent most of her time pursuing black lovers and establishing herself in black social cliques. During her analysis she met a young black professional whom she decided to marry. When the therapist suggested that her plans be delayed until the possible neurotic aspects of her decision could be examined and, if present, resolved, she accused the therapist of being as racist as her parents and siding with them in believing that an interracial marriage is of necessity an expression of psychopathology.

Transference phenomena in the white clients of black therapists are particularly fascinating. On the basis of my familiarity with the literature of psychotherapy and my own professional experiences, I am inclined to believe that recognizable transference phenomena may present themselves more rapidly in white clients when the therapist is black. This is particularly true in the occurrence of dreams in which the therapist appears undisguised. Also because of racial differences, displaced transference phenomena are more readily recognizable in dreams involving blacks or emphasizing color incongruities. With one white male client suffering from chronic schizophrenic deterioration, the first signs of a significant remission in his symptoms coincided with a change in the content of his somatic delusion after several months of treatment with a black therapist. In an almost incidental manner he reported to the therapist that he no longer believed that what had lodged itself in his nose and caused his confusion was a white crystal. He had become convinced then that it was a black cinder. This proved to be an indication that through respiratory introjection the client had incorporated the black therapist into his psychological life and established a workable transference relationship that would make possible his discharge from the back wards of a chronic psychiatric hospital for the first time in many years.

Black Therapist/White Client: Therapist Variables

So far we have focused on client variables in the black therapist/white client relationship. We must turn now to the psychosocial responses of black therapists to interracial therapeutic situations. Obviously, the black therapist will enter treatment relationships with white clients wondering whether he will be accepted by his client and, if so, the extent to which racial differences will complicate what is to transpire. When the black therapist has anxieties about his ability to attract and maintain a white clientele, he may be particularly prone to ingratiating behavior, the gratification of transference wishes, and "acting white." In some cases he may be so conflicted about his black identity that he may subtly convert the therapeutic situation into one in which the white client through reassurance and admiration ends up treating the therapist's neurotic reactions to being black (Curry, 1964b). Or he may be so angry and resentful of racial conditions in the nation that he exhibits the "Crow-Jim phenomenon" wherein he practices reverse racism by requiring of his white clients the strictest adherence to the rules of abstinence and by ruthlessly demanding that they face certain anxiety-producing conflicts before they are adequately prepared to do so. Curry has described the crow-Jim phenomenon as a situation in which animosity, hostility, and bitterness toward whites is experienced by blacks along with a predisposition to injure and discriminate against them. Yet there is evidence (Seward, 1956) indicating that blacks may be particularly effective in work with clients of different ethnic backgrounds.

As in any interracial therapeutic situation, the black therapist is no less required to rid himself of racial hang-ups than whites if he is to be effective in helping his clients. He must deal with racial material in therapeutic situations in a straightforward, objective manner and avoid any inclination to identify individual white clients with whites in general or the negative and oppressive features of our system.

Black Therapist/Black Client: Therapist Variables

Calnek (1970) has written about some of the special difficulties that may develop when black therapists treat black clients. Among the major sources of difficulty, he lists such factors as tendencies in the therapist to deny identification with blacks or to overidentify with them, differential responsiveness to passive versus assertive black clients, class and status differences between therapist and client, and tendencies in upwardly mobile black therapists to view therapeutic work with blacks as low status work and to prefer a white clientele. Sattler (1970) has suggested that in some cases, due to intragroup tension and hostility, black therapists may exhibit less tolerance and understanding of black clients than some white therapists. On the other hand it has been suggested that black clients prefer and work better with black therapists (Sattler, 1970), that black therapists may offer black clients more freedom of expression and an opportunity for deeper identification with black ideals (Seward, 1956), and that black therapists may have an important influence on the development of a healthier ego-ideal in black clients (Kennedy, 1952).

When the black therapist has intense, unresolved conflicts about his own blackness, he may make it difficult for his black clients to deal with their own attitudes about race on their own terms. The black therapist who is strongly identified with conservative-traditional trends in black-white relationships may prefer black clients who are passive, resigned, and masochistic and may reject the more aggressive, militant black client. At the opposite pole are black therapists who are inclined toward militancy and are prone to strong feelings of resentment toward the establishment and toward those blacks who aspire to or actually possess important positions in the establishment. These therapists will show preference for the more militant client and will be inclined to chastise, lecture, or reject the more passive-docile black client (Calnek, 1970).

When the black therapist is free of conflict about his own identity and rightful place in society, he can be of considerable assistance to black clients who need to work out more effective ways of coping with identity problems, racial issues, and the effects of discrimination that have complicated their efforts at successful personal adjustment.

Black Therapist/Black Client: Client Variables

The black client who enters a psychotherapeutic relationship with a black therapist may exhibit considerable anxiety about the therapist's ability to understand his difficulties or to empathize with his view of reality. There may be a tendency to see the therapist's educational attainments and professional status as evidence of identification with whites and rejection of the ways of blacks. In these circumstances the black client may accuse the black therapist of being an "Uncle Tom."

Black clients who themselves reject blackness may, through the projection of their own self-hatred, manifest intense overt hostility toward their black therapist. On the other hand, the more militant black client may accuse the black therapist of having sold out to the white man, of being incapable of understanding the black experience, and of trying to convert blacks to the bourgeois standards and life styles of whites.

Black therapists treating black clients must be prepared to experience many of the same tests by blacks that white therapists are put through. Thus it is as important in their treatment of black clients as it is in their treatment of white clients that the black therapist come to terms with his own feelings about being black in a society that, at deep unconscious levels, considers blacks dirty, unattractive, primitive, and inferior.

Conclusions

The long history of misunderstanding, hostility, and conflict among the races in the United States has had a deep and distorting effect on the systems of ideation and fantasy that are likely to function in interracial relationships. Even in those individuals who experience very little conscious racism, some racial stereotypes will likely continue to exist at unconscious levels and will gain subtle expression in behavior and thought. It could hardly be otherwise considering the nature and history of the black-white relationship in this country.

Stereotypic thinking, difficult to exclude from even our highest intellectual efforts, is demonstrated by the frequency with which research on the psychosocial aspects of race reported in professional journals manifests methodological inadequacy due to failure to control for ethnocentric experimenter bias. Articles appearing in the literature of psychotherapy have been particularly prone to these kinds of errors due to the fact that psychotherapy is "a relatively new discipline which has not yet standardized its concepts, theories and procedures [Doob, 1965]." Nor have training centers, both psychological and psychiatric, given necessary attention to assisting developing professionals in recognizing, understanding, and resolving the more subtle forms that negative attitudes concerning race may take in racially mixed therapeutic relationships.

When we examine psychotherapeutic relationships in forms such as white therapist/black client, black therapist/white client, or black therapist/black client, it is apparent that the topic of race will occupy a place of importance and must be dealt with straightforwardly. Its impact on the therapeutic process itself will vary with the attitudes and personality organizations of both therapist and client. In this chapter I have attempted to discuss some of the more frequent sources of difficulty observed in inter- and intraracial psychotherapy, as well as some specific forms racial conflict and anxiety may take in client and therapist in varying racial combinations. Once these barriers to effective psychotherapy have been dealt with and overcome, the contents and efficacy of therapeutic communication between blacks and whites should differ in no important way from psychotherapy where issues of race do not exist.

References

Adams, W. A. The Negro patient in psychiatric treatment. *American Journal of Orthopsychiatry,* 1950, **20,** 305–310.
Bender, L. Behavior problems in Negro children. *Psychiatry,* 1939, **2,** 213.
Calnek, M. Racial factors in the countertransference: The black therapist and the black patient. *American Journal of Orthopsychiatry,* 1970, **40,** 39–46.
Curry, A. Myth, transference and the black therapist. *Psychoanalytic Review,* 1964, **51,** 7–14.(a)
Curry, A. The Negro worker and the white client. *Social Casework,* 1964, **45,** 131–136.(b)
Doob, L. W. Psychology. In R. A. Lystad (Ed.), *The African world: A survey of social research.* New York: Praeger, 1965.
Greenson, R. R. *The technique and practice of psychoanalysis.* Vol. I. New York: International Universities Press, 1967.
Grier, W. H. When the therapist is Negro: Some effects on the treatment process. *American Journal of Psychiatry,* 1967, **123,** 1587–1582.
Grier W. H., & Cobbs, P. *Black rage.* New York: Basic Books, 1968.
Hamilton, J. Some dynamics of anti-Negro prejudice. *Psychoanalytic Review,* 1966, **53,** 5–15.
Heine, R. W. The Negro patient in psychotherapy. *Journal of Clinical Psychology,* 1950, **16,** 373–376.
Hollingshead, A. B., & Redlich, F. C. *Social class and mental illness: A community study.* New York: Wiley, 1958.
Hunter, D. M., & Babcock, C. G. Some aspects of the intrapsychic structure of certain American Negroes as viewed in the intercultural dynamic. In W. Muensterberger and S. Axelrod (Eds.) *The psychoanalytic study of society,* Vol. IV. New York: International Universities Press, 1967.
Kardiner A., & Ovesey, L. *The mark of oppression.* New York: Norton, 1951.
Kennedy, J. A. Problems posed in the analysis of Negro patients. *Psychiatry,* 1952, **15,** 313–327.
Klineberg, O. *Characteristics of the American Negro.* New York: Harper, 1944.
Rodgers, T. C. The evolution of an active anti-Negro racist. In W. Muensterberger and S. Axelrod (Eds.), *The psychoanalytic study of society,* Vol. I. New York: International Universities Press, 1955.
Rosen, H., & Frank, J. D. Negroes in psychotherapy. *American Journal of Psychiatry,* 1962, **119,** 456–460.
Rosenthal, R. *Experimenter effects in behavioral research.* New York: Appleton-Century-Crofts, 1966.
Sattler, J. M. Racial "experimenter effects" in experimentation, testing, interviewing and psychotherapy. *Psychological Bulletin,* 1970, **73,** 137–160.
Seward G. *Psychotherapy and cultural conflict.* New York: Ronald Press, 1956.
Sommers, U. S. An experiment in group psychotherapy with members of mixed minority groups. *International Journal of Group Psychotherapy,* 1953, **3,** 254–269.

St. Clair, H. R. Psychiatric interview experience with Negroes. *American Journal of Psychiatry,* 1951, **108,** 113–119.

Sterba, R. Some psychological factors in Negro race hatred and in anti-Negro riots. *Psychoanalysis and the Social Sciences,* 1947, **1,** 411–427.

Thomas, A. Pseudo-transference reactions due to cultural stereotyping. *American Journal of Orthopsychiatry,* 1962, **32,** 894–900.

Waite, R. The Negro patient and clinical theory. *Journal of Consulting and Clinical Psychology,* 1968, **32,** 427–433.

Wilson, D. C., & Lantz, E. M. Effect of culture change on the Negro race in Virginia. *American Journal of Psychiatry,* 1957, **114,** 25.

Yamamoto, J., James, O. C., Bloombaum, M., & Hattem, J. Racial factors in patient selection. *American Journal of Psychiatry,* 1967, **124,** 630–636.

Chapter Four

The Black Community's Challenge to Psychology

Norman G. Kerr, Jr.

> Problems of philosophy, ethics, strategy and identity are involved in the challenges that psychology must face in the black community.

It would be meaningful if I first stated this information as background for what will follow. I spend two days of the week as Administrator of the "black program" at Manteno State Hospital. The other three days of the week are spent as Director of The Malcolm X Shabazz Community Mental Health Center, a state-sponsored in-city extension of Manteno Hospital situated on the south side of Chicago. Before discussing the direct and indirect challenges faced by our profession in the black community, let me describe the community and then say something about the mental health services offered by the Malcolm X Center.

Description of the Black Community

The geographical area served by our mental health center is an elongated tract of land extending from Roosevelt Road (12th Street) on the north to 67th Street on the south; from the shores of Lake Michigan on the east to the Dan Ryan Expressway on the west. Those of us who work as mental health professionals within this boundary can bear witness to the stark facts of black urban life in their most paradoxical, most extreme, most crude and brutal form. Let me now present some of these paradoxical facts, not to shock or to confuse you, but to help you to understand the source and environment out of which these facts spring.

According to the latest *Metrozone South Bulletin* (State of Illinois, 1969), the 450,000 or so people who live in this southside area are mostly black and comprise several social classes. There is a small number of financially comfortable upper- and middle-class black and white people who live along Lakeshore Drive in architecturally beautiful high-rise apartments. Farther in from the lake there is a large number of working-class blacks and increasingly large numbers of permanently impoverished underclass black people who have never been able to move to the ranks of the regularly employed, even in marginal occupations. The average yearly income of this underclass group is less than the national poverty level. The number of hungry families has been estimated to be as high as 80,000. The average age at death is significantly less than the national average of 66 years. The infant mortality rate is an astonishing 45 for every 1000 babies born, which is almost three times the national figure. At least 70 percent of the housing is substandard and in various stages of deterioration (Associated Press, February, 1970).

Although there are at least ten state-aided private and public psychiatric clinics and hospitals scattered throughout this southside area, the rate of admission to state mental hospitals is the second highest of any area in Chicago. As to health services, there are three great hospitals in the area with expanding campuses and services (Michael Reese, Mercy, and Billings). Yet statistics indicate that people in this southside community get sick more often, stay sick longer, and die at an earlier age than most people in other areas of Chicago. Even worse, many of the children are often crippled mentally and physically because of the effects of hunger and malnourishment and poor prenatal and postnatal care.

Educationally, this southside area can boast of two famous schools (the University of Chicago and the Illinois Institute of Technology) and a number of good secondary schools such as De LaSalle High School and the Laboratory School of the University of Chicago. Yet public schools designed to prepare children for entry to these secondary schools and universities are dismal failures. For example, there are 50 elementary schools in this area. According to recent reading test scores released by the Chicago Board of Education,

47 out of 50 of these schools contain children who are reading on the average of two years below their eighth-grade-class placement level (Associated Press, January, 1970).

Now it is readily apparent that the aforementioned facts as well as other circumstances create breeding grounds for mental illness and other forms of social pathology on the south side of Chicago. In fact, the experiences of most black people who live in this ghetto are so crude and brutal in quality that the psychological problems generated in their behavior, attitudes, and feelings will likely intensify to the point of mass violence. It is also becoming increasingly clear that our present social and political climate offers little hope for the solution to these problems. Even more to the point of our professional concern, psychologists, as well as other mental health professionals, are poorly trained and ill prepared to address themselves effectively to these problems.

I am painting a pessimistic picture it is true, but we must be realistic if we are ever to overcome our lack of skill, knowledge, and understanding related to the problems of people who live in a state of chronic poverty, dependency, resentfulness, demoralization, and powerlessness.

Organizing a Community Mental Health Service

There have been mental health clinics in the area served by the Malcolm X Community Mental Health Center for well over a decade. However, these agencies were, without exception, imposed on the people without consultation. Their services were geared for verbally fluent patients and there was little interest in or sensitivity to the life styles of inarticulate poor people. As a consequence, services for poor blacks were generally piecemeal, inadequate, and without concern for the dignity of the individual. Moreover, professionals were often discourteous and frequently terminated contacts after the first interview, rationalizing their decision on the "untreatability" of the poor. For these reasons among others, it is little wonder that poor black people have traditionally manifested attitudes of apathy, indifference, and downright hostility toward mental health services.

The way we went about establishing the Malcolm X Community Mental Health Center illustrates an effort to overcome these negative attitudes and to make sure that our clinic would be more responsive to the real needs of the community. Grass-roots people in the community were brought in from the beginning to participate in the planning and the implementation of the mental health programs. It was our advisory council, made up of 20 individuals representing various organizations in the community, that named our clinic after Malcolm X. However, naming the center after a revolutionary leader of poor urban black people would mean little unless we developed innovative methods of delivery that would improve the effectiveness of mental health care and also lead to the development of badly needed programs of prevention.

At the present time we have a staff consisting of social workers, psychiatrists, physicians, psychiatric nurses, nursing assistants, and trainees in psychology and social work. The door of our center is open to the people in the community 24 hours a day, seven days a week, in order to offer diagnostic and treatment services at the time they are needed and in easy reach of those in need.

These are the characteristics of the average patient who seeks our services. An analysis of the records of the last 200 people seen at the Center indicates an age range from six to 85 years, with an average age of 37. Males and females are seen in equal numbers and with few exceptions they are black. He or she is likely to come from a home broken either by divorce, separation, or death. The patient is also likely to be unemployed or underemployed. Educational attainment is about eighth grade. In most cases the patient has been hospitalized more than one time within the past year. The most frequent diagnosis is schizophrenic reaction, paranoid type, followed by depressive reaction and alcoholism. The prognosis is most often guarded and the most frequently recommended treatment is chemotherapy.

Identifying Basic Therapeutic Issues

In the light of the foregoing, certain issues arise for which we are seeking answers. Let me pose some of these questions for you. For example, how can we really help black persons overcome their chronic dependency, inferiority, powerlessness, anger, and depression *without, at the same time, creating new options and opportunities for economic independence* (for example, realistic job training programs)? In short, how can we improve the personality development of a black individual who is forced to live in a brutalizing and degrading slum environment? Therapeutically, we must help black people find constructive release of their internalized anger and resentment and find renewal of hope *through social action programs designed to improve their total condition,* rather than simply empathizing with their hostilities within the therapeutic relationship. What I am really saying is that since we are dealing with people on the lower rungs of the economic ladder who have a multiplicity of unmet social, health, and economic needs, we must attend to the totality of their needs in order to be effective therapeutically. It is not enough merely to dispense a "psychological prescription"; we must establish strong collaborative ties with other community institutions and agencies such as schools, citizen groups, hospitals, medical clinics, social welfare organizations, and the political power structure as well in order to offer comprehensive life-adjustment programs for the patient.

Based on my experience, as a psychologist and administrator in the black community, it is my belief that there are issues much more fundamental than the ones just raised. These have to do with the ideology of the individual psychologist or mental health worker who wants not only to survive in the black community but to accomplish something worthwhile in it as well. The kind of ideology I am speaking about involves a clearly articulated philosophy, a strategy for service, and an identity with the people being served. The important questions of philosophy that enter the picture today are the same ones that Aristotle, Aquinas, Spinoza, Mill, and Freud struggled over—for example, the ageless problem about free will and determinism.

What Psychological Frame of Reference?

In the ghetto, the psychologist who implicitly upholds "free will" may maintain that the patient's psychological problems stem wholly from his own choice or lack of responsibility. Such a premise, however, may lead the psychologist to adopt punitive and rejecting attitudes toward the patient, thus preventing any real understanding of the role of institutionalized social and economic discriminations that affect the patient in ways beyond his control. Moreover, the "it's your own fault" attitude toward the patient precludes the possibility of a meaningful therapeutic relationship. On the other hand, the psychologist with strict deterministic views may adopt overprotective and apologetic attitudes toward the patient, depicting him as a helpless victim of an oppressive socioeconomic system. Because of the need to blame society for the patient's difficulties, the psychologist may be unable to assess realistically the intrapsychic factors that hinder functioning. Whatever position the psychologist takes regarding causality and etiology, its paradoxical and circular character will not let him rest.

Take the question of values. There is documented evidence that the moral standards and cultural beliefs of poor black people differ from the moral values and cultural judgments of middle-class people. What position should the psychologist take on this issue? If his position is that there are absolute moral values and standards of right and wrong that cut across all cultures, his work in the black community will be affected by negative judgmental attitudes. On the other hand, if he decides that there is no way of determining what is good or bad for all people, he may tolerate any behavior in the community as simply reflecting the customs of the culture.

A hot issue in the black community involves obedience to law. For example, should the psychologist encourage the patient to rebel or disobey the civil law when it conflicts with his human rights, or should he take a neutral or opposite position on the question? What should he do if rebellion is resorted to because a majority of people in the black community feel sorely oppressed by the violation of their human rights? What about the related problem of ends and means? Let us suppose that social and economic conditions in the community are bad and oppressive. Should the psychologist encourage or even join his patients in employing any means, nonviolent or violent, in rectifying such conditions? Finally, what is the meaning of freedom for the black man? Should the psychologist support the position of the black power advocates that freedom for blacks means having the power to decide for themselves what they shall do or become and that, therefore, the free black man must be master of himself and not subject at all to the will of whites?

It goes without saying that each psychologist must decide for himself which position he will take. The position he takes, however, will be related to his set of ethics, his treatment strategies, his level of identity with the black community, and his professional effectiveness.

Ethically, for example, is it the responsibility of the psychologist in the black community to be a social activist to the point of marching in a protest parade? Is it his responsibility to be a social activist in the sense of trying to coordinate the functions of social facilities and agencies in order that black people can make the most efficient use of them?

Another ethical question that arises is whether the psychologist has the responsibility to bring home to his black patient the relevance of his present condition in relation to the oppressive system that shapes his life, in order to develop the patient's commitment to confront the system more decisively. If the psychologist takes the position that the patient's problems are a reaction to an abnormal environment created by the power structure, is it ethical to try to have the patient adjust to such a sick society?

Strategically, the psychologist is faced with the problem of developing new approaches to diagnosis and treatment. One may question the appropriateness of diagnostic testing and the validity of present tests in their use with blacks. Some critics are arguing to have all tests banned in the black community until further notice. As to research and evaluation, the black community now takes the position that studies should not be made unless the researchers can guarantee that the results will be of benefit to the people. Treatment-wise, the psychologist is faced with the challenge of experimenting with a variety of techniques such as psychodrama, role playing, sensitivity training, behavior modification, family counseling, hypnotherapy, educational therapy, work therapy, social-action therapy, and the like in order to be successful in the black community.

As to the problem of identity, during this period of history the black community is demanding that blacks work with blacks and that the black psychologist should acknowledge his blackness in terms of black-power ideology. This incorporates an identity with the community along cultural, social, political, and economic lines. Anything less than this is considered a betrayal.

The Crux of the Challenge

Finally, let me make a few comments regarding the black community's challenge to the psychologist as administrator. To understand this challenge, it is necessary to understand the role traditionally occupied by agency or clinic directors in our society. His security has always centered around his identification with the establishment or power structure, and advances that call for radical change in the social system lie outside his concept of reality. In other words, the director has always felt the need to work within the system established by the power structure, and any direct challenge to the system is met by him with anxiety and efforts at repression. The black community is beginning to take the position that the entire community mental health movement is nothing more than a policy of domestic imperialism designed to pacify the natives through tranquilizers, supportive therapies, and other tokens. Further, the community suspects that the director and his staff develop a vested interest in the ghetto as a target for research and as an object of their narcissistic drive to exert control over the lives of a helpless black people.

In light of these factors, the director and his professional staff are being increasingly challenged to choose between maintaining their identity with the establishment and seeking a new identity in support of the people. This is the real challenge that psychology and other disciplines in the mental health field must face.

References

Associated Press, Chicago, Illinois. How median Chicago public schools fared in three national tests. *Chicago Daily News,* January 28, 1970.

Associated Press, Washington, D. C. Health care brutality hit. *Chicago Daily News,* February 23, 1970.

Chicago Tribune Press Service. Filth of Kenwood told Senate group. *Chicago Tribune,* February 20, 1970.

State of Illinois Department of Mental Health. *Chicago's Metrozone South Bulletin, Subzone 11 Planning,* 1969.

Part Three

From the Lives of Black Psychologists

Chapter Five
Looking Back on Growing Up Black

Thomas J. Edwards

Blacks who have grown up in the United States have different amounts and different kinds of psychological scar tissue. It is doubtful that any black American is totally free from this scarring. As we became scarred in different ways, so we have our own unique and private ways of reacting to the slings and arrows of outrageous racism. Human experience and personal adaptation are always unique. The uniqueness of each black man's personality organization determines the uniqueness of his responses to growing up black in these United States.

Our American society places a high premium on the rags-to-riches phenomenon. It's the log-cabin-to-the-White-House syndrome. If you have come from a lowly beginning and have "made it," your story is worth telling. Our game of one-upmanship awards brownie points for having had it tough as a youth. The story of my life holds its own in this regard rather well, but these are things about me that I seldom reveal.

I qualify for membership in the black rags-to-riches ingroup because Mom was a domestic servant and Pop was a janitor at the public school in my hometown. We were poor. I must admit, however, that I did not grow up in an urban black ghetto. Sociologists make such a big thing about black ghettos that those of us who grew up in ordinary small communities feel slighted. We were not denied our share of second-classness.

I also qualify for membership in the black rags-to-riches ingroup because daily in a thousand subtle ways my community conveyed to all of its blacks the message that superior status in the local pecking order was based on pigmentation deficiency. The North has traditionally looked down its nose with contempt at the antiblack laws and mores below the Mason-Dixon Line. However, we all know that the Deep South had no monopoly on racism. Psychological scar tissue due to experiences of rampant racism is not absent from blacks born and reared in the Deep North.

I learned the lessons of inferior black status at an early age in our suburban Philadelphia community. Until I was 12 years old, for example, blacks were required to sit on the right side down front in our only movie theater. We were so conditioned to being treated with this special derogatory distinction that most blacks continued to occupy the Jim-Crow section of this theater even after Pennsylvania passed its equal-rights law. As a young quasi-militant, I tried to persuade my mother to sit in the center section, but she refused, insisting that she could not see well from the center. This pathetic response illustrates the erosion of confidence and security in society and the permanent psychological defensiveness generated in blacks by their experiences of discrimination.

A few blocks from our house through the woods, the Media Swimming and Boating Club was on the shores of a pleasant lake. Its membership was "private," a classification we black youths recognized all too well as merely a ruse to keep us out. We knew that our white schoolmates were able to join. To a degree we resigned ourselves to these indignities as a way of life, much as if it were a part of a white "Divine Plan." Yet we did rebel. On many a hot summer night we would race down through the woods, strip completely, plunge into the lake, and pollute the sacred waters of the whites with our glistening black bodies. This defiance was a delight. But in the silent depths of our beings we suffered the tragedy of the black experience in America.

School was at that stage of the game an essentially irrelevant experience for me. The silent—but not too silent—message communicated to me was of a destiny to grow up and become a black adult and a black menial. Blacks in our community did not go to college. Our black models were laborers and domestic servants for white people. What then was the relevance of learning the dull task of diagramming sentences? What was the point of trying to achieve academic excellence? So I went through school cafeteria-style, picking and choosing an occasional goody, but remaining a solid D+ student. I doubt that any but a negligible few of us black pupils were aware of possessing any significant learning capacity. And what if we did?

So our level of aspiration was markedly depressed. We set few goals, and most of these were directed toward hedonism and survival. I was to be a competent servant, a cook, and a butler. My mother gave me excellent basic training in each of these arts, and in my mid-teens they were my major sources of income. I resented my lot in life.

Once a white lady for whom I was a houseboy left me a note of instructions for the chores I was to perform. I completed them quickly, failing to realize that there were instructions on both sides. Gleeful at being through with my tasks and free to do the forbidden thing of roaming about the house, I went into the living room and began to play the piano. Shortly the door opened, and in walked my irate employer-lady. My work was only half done! I had taken liberties in the house! I was in trouble! Why did I have to be a blasted servant, anyway!

Despite what seemed to be our black doom, there was never a total resignation to the status of inferiority. The experiences that kept hope alive were individual, unique, and often born of fortuitous events. Accidentally, I learned that speaking a foreign language was easy for me and that it was exciting and fun. But I also learned that a black youth who could speak a foreign language was an enigma to whites, a confusing contradiction of the stereotypic inarticulate, simpleminded darky, unable even to speak standard American.

It all started when I was 14 and was working as a delivery boy in an Italian grocery store. My hometown had a rather large Sicilian community and many of these Italians came to the store to shop and to visit a bit. I listened to the stream of Italian with fascination. Soon I began asking how this or that was said in Italian. I developed a working vocabulary rather rapidly, mastered the pronunciation, inferred something of the rules of grammar, and learned to read and write Italian. When Pepi Gallo or Zio Pietro Pizzuro came shopping or visiting, I would chat with them. I learned to sing "Santa Lucia" in Italian.

The most significant experiences were on Saturday nights. The store would be crowded with weekly shoppers, and as I put new stock up on the shelves, I would babble away with Italians, much to the confusion of the non-Italian customers. Their confusion delighted me because I was learning that my newfound language facility was one weapon I could use against the preconceived racist attitudes of whites.

Later when I was 16 and in high school, I studied Latin and German. Across the street from our school there was a German bakery shop. I wanted a second language weapon against white bigotry, but I was not quite confident. During the Christmas season I threw open the door of the German bakery shop and yelled "Fröhliche Weihnacht und glückliches neues Jahr!" (Merry Christmas and Happy New Year) and fled. Some time later I collected courage and five cents, and dared to enter the bakery shop. I bought a cream-filled doughnut and greeted Mrs. Guggenheim in schoolboy German. She was warmly pleasant and responded in slow, clear German. I had made it! This was the point of no return! My linguistic saber was whetted and I was ready.

Daily I went to the bakery at lunchtime and after school. I learned idioms, attuned my ear to correct pronunciation, and bluffed my way through the impossible 16 cases of German. I could chat glibly with my German teacher, but I was still a solid D+ student in German because I went to the bakery shop instead of doing my homework. Learning the principle parts of German verbs was dull, and what did I care as long as I passed? I was to be a domestic servant, so my grades would not matter. But my weapon of language was steadily sharpening, and I could slash into whitey's stereotype of a black at the drop of an umlaut.

One summer I helped clean during the annual two-week shutdown at a paper mill. I recall vividly being up on a stepladder wiping off the pipes in the research lab, rag in hand, when I chanced to peer down at a white chap about my age who was struggling with a hefty tome entitled *Papier Fabrik* (Paper Factory). A dictionary was beside him, and he was laboriously translating the technology of the German paper manufacturing industry into English. I greeted him casually and climbed down from my perch, wipe rag still in hand. Rather quickly, and with covert condescension, I helped him over several rough spots of German syntax and vocabulary.

There were two reactions to this experience. First, I had scored a black victory for myself by exhibiting superior competence in an area in which whites fancied themselves to be superior. However, there remained the gnawing question: Why, in spite of my victory, was I doomed by being black to a fate just a cut above my ancestor's who were slaves? This was the dilemma that black psychic scar tissue was made of.

There was still another language weapon that I had but had neglected to realize and to use with effect. It was the language we spoke at home comfortably and without affectation. This was my native dialect, which I had taken so for granted that I did not realize that it too could be a powerful ace-in-the-hole. My own language had simply served as a means of communication. No big deal. But now, suddenly, it became a significant device for self-administered psychotherapy in my attempts to solve the problems of being black in these United States. I began to write prolifically, vomiting up the indigestible chunks of my black experience. At the age of 16 I wrote a poem entitled "Born Black."

> I's never done no wrong,
> Jes born black;
> But treated like a hunted beast
> What is it that I lack?
>
> I tries to do what's right, God knows;
> But 'cause my skin is dark,
> I's shoved back in de corner
> With kinky hair my mark.
>
> 'Tain't always gonna be that way.
> My Master's voice I'll hark,
> Then climb up to a higher place.
> God loves me though I'm dark.

Unable to cope with possible here-and-now solutions to the problem of being born black in my native land, I could see only death and a kind, patronizing, understanding white god as the ultimate surcease to my pain.

Standard American English served its purpose, too. I did not give a damn about academic achievement per se, but I did want to confound the establishment—my white peers and my white teachers. So I began writing for the school newspaper and became its literary editor! One of my editorials entitled "Black Youth" began: "Being sixteen is an amazing experience. It's like being in a forest on a sunny spring day when the process of rejuvenation is just beginning...." But having described the common experience of 16 year-olds, I proceeded to spell out the special problems of the black teenager. The black students responded with quiet applause. White teachers were approving. I do not recall any reactions from white classmates. Perhaps none were voiced. But I felt better.

Then there was the hometown weekly newspaper. Somehow I managed to get my articles accepted. I wrote straight news, obituaries, editorials, sports, and ultimately a feature column. This feature column was to serve as another weapon against the feelings of complacent superiority of the white community. Each week I did a character sketch of a well-known personality in our hometown. But I always alternated—one week a black, the next week a white. This was years before black youths dared to be outwardly militant, so my tactics were accordingly studied and insidious.

Black Americans used to learn to hate their blackness early. It was ugly because it was not Caucasian. It was our badge of rejectability. So how could a black youth handle this rejection of blackness—this self-rejection—when it came to his female-directed urges and the selection of a mate?

I again retreated into the therapy of writing. I wrote "Black Maiden."

> Black maiden, thou art as a garden flower,
> Half-way concealed by some marauding parasite.
> Thy darkness keeps thy purity within thy soul
> And hides thy chastity from common sight.
>
> And as some prickly rose is decked with thorns,
> Lest man should pluck whene'er his way leads past,
> God made thee black but put a soul within,
> Thus thou retain thy purity steadfast.

This poem reveals much about the psychosexual problems of growing up black in the United States. Why did I have to explain or forgive or justify a God who created some of his maidens with the curse of blackness?

What seems now like eons ago, I recall walking to school with Jack, a white schoolmate who lived a block away, but on the "white end" of Fifth Street. We often walked to and from school together. Jack got As on his report card, had respectable hopes and aspirations, and had reasons to hope and to aspire. Although I maintained my solid D+ average, I was Jack's intellectual peer and held my own in our walk-to-school dialogues. I remember that when we were about 11 years old we discussed the race problem. I told him (and I'll never know just how I knew it then) that my life would be far richer because of the struggle forced on me on account of my blackness. This was a prophetic out-of-the-mouths-of-babes thing.

Two of us in the cast of our senior play were black. We were the menials of course, but we refused to play our roles in dialect. We never missed a rehearsal and the whole production was fun, and as we got better and better toward the night of dress rehearsal, we were euphoric. But then came the unexpected but, I guess, inevitable denouement. The leading man had a little cast party and invited everyone except the two of us who were black. What a painful anticlimax, and again the stuff of which black psychic scar tissue is made.

Then there was the second great war to end all wars, and off we went to serve in segregated or semisegregated branches of the service. I was a sailor. In boot camp we were in totally segregated units. Integration was to come later. At my second base, Ellis Island, while we awaited reassignment, I saw a notice one day on the bulletin board: "Anyone interested in the Navy V-12 program contact Mr. Amati in the Personnel Office." What a great opportunity! By then I had one-and-a-half years of college. I bounded up the stairs. But Mr. Amati was all apologies. He explained that I could not qualify because I was pigmented. A war to make the world safe for democracy.

Growing up black in America results in the development of certain response tendencies that operate at a reflex level and at times may seem inappropriate. For example, we blacks characteristically display what I often refer to as "minority paranoia." We are frequently suspicious of whites whom we do not know well, and even after we have gotten to know them well, a tendency to remain slightly on guard often remains. Related to this phenomenon of minority paranoia is the sprouting of invisible defensive antennas that are long and extraordinarily sensitive. These antennas pick up minute clues emanating from comments or gestures and alert us to the degree of guardedness or defensiveness that we sense is necessary in our interactions with a given white individual. Admittedly there are times when we blacks misread the intent of whites as racist. But I contend that these occasional misreadings are far less handicapping than it would be for us to pull in these antennas and make ourselves more vulnerable to the racial trauma that is still inevitable from time to time.

It often amazes me that blacks have not suffered from an even higher incidence of emotional disorder and suicide. This is as inexplicable as the fact that the vast majority of blacks shunned communism, fought in several ridiculous wars, and remained loyal to this country despite the nature of the black experience here. In part, the effects of that experience of enslavement conditioned many of our forefathers to docility and resignation out of fear and a feeling of powerlessness. The establishment was viewed as a formidable and unshakable monolith. Years of brainwashing about our alleged inferiority convinced many of us that our inferiority was a fact. Thus the attitudes of resignation and "why fight it?" However, mixed with this resignation was a gnawing unrest and a corresponding need for fulfillment. Much of the music, language idioms, writing, and other products of black American culture reflect this unrest in blacks and our will to overcome. Better to sing the blues than to rave in psychosis.

But the black experience in America is changing. Whereas those of us blacks who grew up much before the present will have to take our psychological scars to our graves, contemporary and future generations of young blacks growing up in this country will have a different kind of experience and a healthier sense of self. The history and sociology of the developments of this era, which are creating the new black, will be significant for all time. The process is a reality—a phenomenon that has progressed to a point of no return.

I look at the future of the black experience in America with an optimism that some may indeed regard as unfounded. My philosophy may spring partly from an urgent need for a sense of hope that I must nourish if I am to function at all in this society.

Chapter Six
The Making and Breaking of a Black Soldier*

It was February, 1946. I stood on deck of the Costa Rica Victory as it ploughed toward land. The guardian of New York harbor began to emerge from the mist holding high her torch of enlightenment and liberty. The troops were straining in ecstasy at the railings. The white ones, that is. I was numb with ambivalence. My numbness grew as that statue grew in front of me with every turn of the Victory's screws.

Was it really over? Had I really survived the unknown two years in Europe and the five campaigns of the war that had once been ahead of me? Had I survived the strain of surviving emotionally as a black soldier in a white man's army? The call had been close on all counts.

Almost three years earlier on a hot June day in Fort Lewis, Washington, the dust was being stirred by every gust of breeze. This same dust mixed with the winter's rains would make us dub this place "Fort Mud Hole." A courier from Battalion Headquarters rushed up with a sense of urgency and interrupted me. I was policing the grounds of cigarette butts with a pin-pointed stick. The interruption was welcomed, because after three days of this duty since my arrival, I felt sure that someone would become curious to see if I could be

---

*This account is autobiographical and the events are told essentially as they occurred. Only the names of persons have been altered.

of greater service to the Quartermaster Corps. However, I was surprised and nervous that the summons came from Battalion Headquarters. Lieutenant Wakefeld, the battalion adjutant, ordered me to report immediately.

He sat behind his desk hardly recognizing my still awkward salute as I stood at attention, uneasy about looking like a tramp in my dusty, baggy fatigues. Slowly and crisply he said, "Private Pugh, your *Form 20* says here that you are a graduate of Ohio State University." "That's right, sir," I replied. "Where is Arps Hall located on the campus?" he demanded. I explained where the building was situated, but was puzzled by the question. Then he wanted to know where the library was located. I told him. By this time it was clear that Wakefeld was testing my knowledge of the Ohio State campus. He had made up his mind before ever seeing me that I had possibly lied on an official army document! He leaned forward and his eyes narrowed as he shot out, "What happened on commencement day, June, 1941?" I explained that, just as the line of march entered the stadium, a downpour scattered the guests and the 1601 graduates, that not many of us could get near the makeshift ceremony put together under the grandstands, and that an announcement was made that our diplomas would be sent to us by mail. He continued to stare at me for a minute. Then gradually, as if reluctantly, his expression relaxed and he began to accept the fact that this black soldier could have received a master's degree in psychology at that commencement. "Private Pugh, I was also in that commencement," he informed me. Then pointedly, "I received my bachelor's degree that day." I stiffened. He ordered me to duty as a clerk-typist in the Headquarters Detachment under his command.

A thousand black recruits had been sent to Fort Lewis to receive basic training and to form this quartermaster battalion. A number of low-ranking noncoms had been returned from Hawaii as cadre, and if all went well for them they would become the top-ranking noncommissioned officers of the battalion. Two of them would even become warrant officers and by that would gain about the same privileges as the commissioned officers, all of whom were white. The commissioned officers were also looking forward to the elevations in rank that their new assignments called for—if all went well. So everybody was new in his position, everybody had to prove himself, and everybody was bucking for promotion.

Wakefeld was a first lieutenant, but as battalion adjutant and commander of the Headquarters Detachment he was slated to become a captain. From the outset it was plain—very plain—that he had no intention of letting anything get in the way of his promotion, which, I am sure, he saw as just the next step toward a much higher goal. As adjutant, he was the keeper and guardian of all the records. He had gone over the records of each of the 1000 recruits and had carefully selected the most intelligent and the best educated for his Headquarters Detachment of about 16 men. He lived strictly by *Army Regulations* plus certain of his own rules, and no one under his command was to deviate from them. Wakefeld was an automaton of efficiency.

Major McDaniel, who was to be our commander, was among the last to arrive, and we all expectantly fell out for his first battalion formation, officers and enlisted men. He had a ruddy, wrinkled neck and a deep Texas drawl. He announced that he was a regular army man, had come up through the ranks, and was proud to have done this without going past the sixth grade. Under his guidance, he declared, we would all become real soldiers to make ourselves and our country proud. There would be no excuses and no complaints from "any living ——."

As he talked, it was obvious that his dentures were giving him trouble. He finally jerked out the uppers. There he stood before his battalion, a fine soldier, akimbo with legs apart, his dentures in one hand, and punctuating the remainder of his directives by scratching his crotch with the other. That was to become a disgustingly familiar scene.

What we enlisted men did not guess then was something Major McDaniel knew all too well: he had sunk about as low as a field officer could get in the United States Army when he was assigned the command of a raw black quartermaster battalion. But the payoff for him would be a lieutenant-colonelcy—if all went well.

So for better or worse, there I was, and I felt that the best thing I could do was to mind my own business and do my job by the numbers. In other words, my front became impeccably GI. However, for the first time in my life I started grinding my teeth in my sleep. This tension symptom became progressively worse over the next year until my jaws would ache after I awoke in the mornings. I first became aware of doing this when the fellows who slept near me complained of mice making noise in the barracks. The "mice" turned out to be my teeth crunching together.

Hopefully, since I had all the qualifications, my escape hatch would be Officer Candidate School. I applied for the Adjutant

General's OCS, which would allow me to serve as a psychologist—and waited. Other men applied for OCS or ASTP (Army Specialized Training Program)—and waited. Little did we know that the wait would be long and in vain. Not one man got to OCS or ASTP from that outfit during the entire war.

One day we received the news that the guy who had been retained for two weeks in the post hospital and had been the center of confusion for the post commander and his staff was finally going to be assigned to our Headquarters Detachment. Everybody was curious about how this dude would fit in. The point of confusion was that he had refused to declare himself either black or white. Every time he had to declare his racial identity, he would say he was Portuguese. He had been born in the United States, but his parents were Portuguese. The problem with Tony Diego was that his skin was just a little too brown, his glistening black hair was too tightly curled, and his features were just slightly too Negroid. Therefore, he had been evaluated for two weeks in the post hospital by army medical officers and was finally declared by them to be black.

Tony Diego fitted in beautifully. He turned out to be a likable guy who would never discuss his episode in the post hospital. But his look of quiet amusement whenever we asked about it suggested that he had derived some kind of personal satisfaction from it all. Tony became one of my best friends.

Wakefield began to depend on me, which meant that in his own way he warmed up to me. He was obviously impressed by the only thing he could ever respect in anybody: my conscientiousness and hard work. He had seemingly no capacity to respond to the human factor, and he was as completely authoritarian as anyone I have ever known. One day he issued orders giving me the two stripes of a Technician, Fifth Grade. This made me the first recruit to get a promotion. Part of my new assignment included some classroom teaching connected with the basic training program. In addition, I was to make a weekly intelligence report concerning troop morale and any other observations about the outfit that I considered important. This report was mailed directly and secretly to a special army intelligence office without crossing either Wakefield's or McDaniel's desk. However, even though I never knew for sure, I always suspected that the reports were routed back to them, at least in summary form.

Morale deteriorated progressively. Wakefield's expectations and demands were excessive. McDaniel's arrogant ignorance was revolting and unproductive of the performance he needed from the men to make him look good. His solution was to bear down harder. A covert, vicious struggle was generated between the white officers and the black recruits. The officers were sure they would win in the end. After all, they had complete authority over the men, and their army careers were at stake. Interestingly and inevitably, the more their methods defeated their purposes, the more tenaciously they applied them.

Then came the final test of the success of basic training: maneuvers. Ours were to be on the Oregon desert.

Truck after truck churning up the desert's lava bed. Living in dust masks. Scorching temperatures at the height of the day, and water turning to ice overnight. Each day moving the entire headquarters—tents, files of records, typewriters, tables, everything. And of course there were the big tents with cots for the officers to sleep in. We slept on the ground in pup tents. And, of course, there was the officers' latrine, which a detail had to dig each day and make private with a specially erected canvas. The smelly pine box with its appropriately spaced holes to support those special white buttocks had its own reserved place in the truck on the move. Our black buttocks strained over an open slit trench always located a most appropriate distance away.

At the end of one long hard day we arrived at our designated bivouac area just a little before dusk. Wakefeld had been delayed, and we were anxious to get the headquarters tents pitched and everything set up before dark. Since we had done it time after time by now, the top sergeant gave orders to proceed after some thoughtful hesitation. With the required strain, speed, and sweat, we had things in order just at dark and were ready to start pitching our own pup tents so we could finally collapse. Just then Wakefeld's jeep drove up and screeched to a stop. He jumped out and screamed, "Who ordered those tents pitched?" Hodge, our top sergeant, nervously admitted responsibility, trying to explain why he had gone ahead. Others of us spoke up in his support. Wakefeld, livid, informed us that *he* was the commander of the Headquarters Detachment, and he ordered us to strike every tent, move every piece of equipment exactly one foot to the east, and repitch the tents. That was the last time old Master Sergeant Hodge, who had made it from the cadre, ever attempted to exercise initiative. From then on he opted to assume the servile attitude for survival that he had learned so well in dealing with whites during his growing up years in Florida.

Returning from maneuvers enroute to Fort Lewis, Wakefeld

assigned me to drive his jeep. We were moving at night in stark blackout conditions, following the "cat's eyes" of the vehicle ahead. Soon Wakefeld was asleep. His body slumped over and his head fell on my shoulder where it remained for eons. Ye gods!

The news was unbelievable. I had never heard of an outfit —an entire battalion—flunking its basic training; but that was the startling decision of the reviewing team from higher headquarters. McDaniel in defeat was enraged and saw his lt.-colonelcy vanishing in thin air. Wakefeld was beside himself with frustration after working so hard for his captaincy. The entire battalion had to repeat much of its basic training. Conditions for obtaining passes and leave became almost impossible. Now *our* war really became hell!

Wakefeld's new ruling was that if any man in Headquarters Detachment was delinquent in any respect under any circumstance, no man in the Headquarters could have a pass or leave. At the end of the work day no one could leave his desk in Battalion Headquarters until every man there had finished his day's assignment. If one man did not pass his barracks inspection with bed, footlocker, and gear intact, every man would be restricted. Wakefeld, who was about five feet five, inspected the rafters for dust by having someone lift him by his stiffened legs to within finger-swiping reach of the two-by-fours.

My secret letters to that mysterious intelligence office had long since been warning of serious problems due to dangerously low morale in the battalion. However, for fear that McDaniel and Wakefeld finally saw the reports, I exercised great care to be vague about the apparent causes, placing the blame on no one specifically. I only hoped that someone, somewhere, might finally take my reports seriously and do something. Although I and every other enlisted man were just about to a breaking point, this was all I could think to do up to that time. However, just about then I had to take another serious blow to my own hopes for escape. I heard a rumor, which was only too easy to believe, that the Adjutant General's OCS had never accepted a black candidate. At any rate, I never received a response to my application and never knew why.

McDaniel's hopes for those silver oak leaves of the lieutenant colonel grew thin. Deep down he must have realized that he was a man alone, respected by no one—neither his officers nor his men—although everybody was bound to pay him respect. Mostly he was hostile and arrogant. But sometimes when he was obviously under the influence of liquor he even tried the backslapping let's-be-pals approach with his officers. But not with Wakefeld. He hated Wakefeld almost innately; nevertheless, he knew how dependent he was on his adjutant. After all, the shape of the battalion records and the mechanical efficiency of the headquarters office were the two things McDaniel could always count on and brag about.

But having discovered Wakefeld's sore point—his central vulnerability—McDaniel could not at times resist rubbing salt in the wound. "Where does that name of yours come from, Wakefeld? Hosea Wakefeld—what a name! Well, answer me!" he'd bark. "What'sa matter, huh? You ashamed of being Jewish? Huh? Maybe he's scared of Hitler!"

Wakefeld took those insults in silence, but it was clear by his attitude that he was enraged by McDaniel and also that he was quite ashamed of being Jewish. However, he would never say anything that might jeopardize his chances for getting those shiny double bars, and as long as McDaniel was his commander, McDaniel controlled those chances.

Then it happened.

The wives of a couple of the men came to visit them, fearing that we would be shipped overseas without leave home because of our extended training time. A corporal in the Medics named Morse had become a proud father for the first time after he had been inducted, and he was eager to see his son. Morse was a rather quiet and shy man who was planning to study for the ministry when the war was over. He had arranged for his wife and child to come and spend a few days in Tacoma, Washington, the nearest town, but he was so afraid that Wakefeld might not let him spend time off the post with his family that he was virtually in an anxiety state. Wakefeld surprised everybody, however, and showed little resistance to Morse's having a weekend pass; but even though his wife and child were to leave on Monday afternoon, Wakefeld stipulated that Morse would have to report back for duty at eight o'clock on Monday morning and work until it was time for him to put his family on the train for home. For this he would have to secure another pass.

Morse returned on time, happy from his weekend. All of us thought, however, that it was ridiculous for him to have to forego those last few hours with his wife and child. But he put in his work and reported to Wakefeld for the second pass when the time came. Wakefeld looked up from his desk with the pass in his hand and scrutinized Morse for a minute. Then he said sarcastically, "Corporal, do you realize that you have a button missing from your jacket?" "Yes, sir, I do," Morse answered nervously, and quickly added, "but my wife is going to sew it on before she leaves." Then there was silence. Wakefeld spoke again: "Because you are improperly dressed, corporal, your pass is denied!"

All the men stopped dead in their tracks. We could not believe our ears. Morse begged Wakefeld to reconsider because his wife could not easily manage her luggage and the baby in boarding a train, plus she would be worried sick if he failed to show.

Wakefeld was adamant. At that moment he became the most unreasonable and hateful man that I ever hope to have the misfortune to know. All of us were dumbfounded, especially because Morse had been an exemplary soldier and had never before received a demerit of any kind.

Tension could be cut with a knife, and we were about to explode when, with a voice quivering with emotion, Morse said, "I'm sorry, Lt. Wakefeld, but I'm going to see my family to the railroad station." He saluted, turned, and walked out of the office.

Somebody had finally done it! Somebody had finally drawn the line and asserted his sense of integrity, and the guy who had done it was the quietest and most unassuming man in the Detachment. Within hours, Morse was reduced from corporal to private and had a sizeable fine imposed by courtmartial.

For me, the dam had broken. For the sake of my own integrity I knew I would have to make a move. I could no longer participate in this insanity without protest and maintain my own sanity or any semblance of self-respect. Still it was difficult for me to accept that the situation was beyond any constructive solution. I went to Hodge, urging him as top sergeant to speak to Wakefeld for the sake of the men under him and for his own sake, because our situation was now intolerable and no relief was in sight. But Hodge had had it. It was no more than I had expected when he rationalized not doing it "for fear of making things worse," because he did not think there was a chance of making them better. I understood Hodge very well. What he meant was that he was not willing to take a self-respecting stand and to gain the respect of his men for fear of jeopardizing the six stripes that were his life's greatest achievement. But at least I had respected him and had not gone over his head. He gave me permission to approach Wakefeld myself.

By this time, I had been promoted to staff sergeant and was the fourth ranking enlisted man in the Headquarters Detachment and was the highest ranking of all the men in the battalion who had been recruits. I was outranked only by Hodge and the two technical sergeants, all from the cadre. So I had worked hard, had been extremely patient, and had done well for myself under the circumstances. But all this had been accomplished at an extreme price emotionally, and the payoff had ceased to be worth the cost. Also, I somehow sensed that Wakefeld and McDaniel thought that my success would serve to keep me in line, and that in spite of everything else I would be grateful to them because few enlisted men had risen so fast up the noncommissioned ladder. They were also very much aware of my hopes for OCS; but in looking back, I feel that by this time they knew very well that my hopes would be in vain. However, I was still clinging to the chance that my break might come any day, even up to the time our outfit might receive orders to go overseas. So I knew what was at stake for me, but I had to make the move. I decided to risk presenting my view of things to Wakefeld.

I caught Wakefeld alone and told him that I had a request to make. He was immediately curious and asked what it was. I said that I had something very serious to discuss with him and that I preferred that we meet under circumstances where we could talk man-to-man and forget our military ranks—that he was a first lieutenant and that I was a staff sergeant. I requested to see him in his private quarters, after hours, at his convenience, if he would.

Wakefeld was obviously stunned but contained himself, as usual. There was apprehension in his eyes, but his face was stern and his voice was firm when, after only a moment's hesitation, he replied, "O.K. I'll see you tonight in my quarters at eight o'clock sharp."

I knocked on his door at exactly eight. He asked me in and indicated that I should sit down. I sat on the edge of a chair, and he sat opposite me. We were both tense and uncomfortable. Wakefeld's movements were rigid, revealing that his defenses were up. This was going to be difficult, but I had to try to reach him. I was convinced it was the one thing left to try if we were to achieve a more constructive turn of events for the men who comprised the small Headquarters Detachment, and perhaps for all the other enlisted men in the battalion. I knew for certain it was the only hope for me.

I began with a slow and thoughtful review of the sequence of events as I had observed and experienced them from the day I had been called from policing the grounds to be assigned to Battalion Headquarters under his command. I noted that he had selected the best-qualified men from among a thousand recruits for his Headquarters Detachment. I stated that these men had measured up to expectations rather well in my opinion, as attested to by the amount of work they turned out and the efficient operation of the headquarters office. As I saw it, these men were conscientious and hard-working but human and certainly not beyond fault; they wanted to succeed in every way they could and basically had no desire to create a difficult situation deliberately either for others or for themselves. At its very best, being in the service in a time of war was difficult enough for anyone. Nevertheless, human beings can sustain their efforts best when they are respected as human beings and when they feel some appreciation and receive some reward for their efforts. I said that in my opinion the battalion's debacle on maneuvers and failure, therefore, to qualify for overseas duty was a pure reflection of a serious morale problem. It was my firm belief, I continued, that these men, as well as any group of men under similar circumstances, would respond to appreciative leadership; however, I as well as others of us were puzzled by the fact that from the very beginning, instead of appreciative leadership, we had essentially experienced being mercilessly driven.

Wakefeld heard all this in stony silence. I had stopped because I could see that I was not getting through; but I was still not prepared for the extreme response I got.

"Is that what you came here to say?" he asked.

"That is the gist of it at least, sir," I replied.

Then angrily, Wakefeld continued. "Well, I have just one thing to say to all that. You asked to talk with me man-to-man, and I'll answer you man-to-man. It's simply that *Negroes have to be driven in order to be led!*"

Now *I* was stunned. I felt hopeless and angry, and the only thing that mattered to me from then on was what I said to him. "Well, sir, if this is your attitude and if this is the only response you can make to what I have tried to do, I feel I can no longer do my best here and I no longer wish to serve under your command. Tomorrow morning I shall submit in writing a request for transfer to any other outfit in the United States Army, regardless of the circumstances."

"And your request will be denied," he replied.

My request *was* summarily denied, but I was sure that my days were numbered. Wakefeld would not be so kind as to do it my way at my request—he would eventually do it his way and to his complete satisfaction.

The days were rapidly approaching Christmas. Finally, the battalion made the grade and passed its basic training. One morning

Wakefeld appeared sporting the double silver bars of a captain, making little effort to hide his pride. Shortly thereafter the table of organization was just about complete, and all the promotions for officers and enlisted men had been accomplished but one. McDaniel was still a major.

At long last, a leave list was completed and the men began going home. We were truly fortunate that it all came at that time of year, because we felt certain that it would be the last time we would see our homes and loved ones for a long time to come. I had my leave at Christmas, still sporting the four stripes of the staff sergeant. When I arrived home, it was like emerging from some horrible nightmare. After a couple of nights and for the rest of the leave, on waking in the mornings my jaws were not so achy anymore.

By the time all the men were back from leave, the winter rains set in at Fort Lewis. It drizzled for 12 days without stopping and turned the place into "Fort Mud Hole." There was a feeling in the air that something was brewing—we were issued all new equipment; gear was inspected and reinspected; our carbines were oiled and polished, checked and rechecked. The officers relaxed their attitudes; even Wakefeld and McDaniel softened a little. The men welcomed this relief but were wary and suspected that the officers were beginning to be concerned about finding themselves in combat with a bunch of angry men. It was commonly whispered around the battalion, "Just let me find one of those sons-a-bitches with his butt in front of my rifle in combat!" We were now as ready as we would ever be, and we were impatient to get out of there and get it over with.

The move started one morning when Wakefeld announced that an advanced cadre of four men, two officers and two enlisted men, was to leave immediately, and that the battalion would follow in due time. The destination and time elements were, of course, a secret. Wakefeld himself was not to be a part of this advanced cadre, but he selected me as one of the enlisted men for this important job, and I was surprised. In spite of everything, Wakefeld still depended on me.

After we boarded the train, it was not too long before we guessed that we were probably headed for the East coast, which meant that we would likely end up in Europe. I was relieved and happy about that prospect. For me better Europe than the Far Pacific, because seeing Europe for free would be a valuable compensation for all else that had to be endured.

After a fantastic 24-hour leave in New York City, we left Camp Shanks under cover of night and boarded an oceangoing vessel that seemed endless in every dimension. It just about was, for it was the Queen Elizabeth, decked out as a troop ship. In addition to the crew, we were told that there were 16,000 soldiers aboard, and from my vantage point there was no reason whatsoever to question that estimate.

I distinctly remember feeling awed and happy about this first "foreign" experience—the opportunity to cross the Atlantic aboard the world's largest and most famous ship. Somehow I also had expected an immediate change for the better for us black American servicemen once we got involved in any foreign experience. However, that expectancy was short-lived and I had a rude awakening to the British attitude toward blacks when we went down to breakfast the next morning.

On boarding we had been assigned quarters and were given a ticket indicating when and where we were to take our meals. The quarters were comfortable enough under the circumstances—three three-tiered bunks in a stateroom with bath. We were much more fortunate than some others who had to camp on the open deck. However, our quarters were below the water level and could become a death trap if the ship were torpedoed.

There were just 40 black soldiers on board out of the estimated 16,000 troops. It so happened that we were all parts of small advanced cadres for a number of different black outfits. Of the 40 I would estimate that about four were warrant officers and the rest of us were noncoms. The four black warrant officers were segregated in quarters by themselves among the officers, and the remaining 36 of us black noncoms were segregated in quarters from the other 15,000 and some white enlisted men aboard!

When we showed up at the mess hall for our first meals, the British mess crew tried to get us to sit at tables they had segregated from the rest. That was too much. We just refused to do it, and we continued to refuse until it became too difficult a situation for them to control because of the continual throng being served almost around the clock. They finally gave up trying. How incredible that anyone would go to such extreme efforts and bookkeeping in order to segregate so few human beings from so many! However, this was merely our introductory experience to British prejudice toward blacks during World War II.

The Elizabeth pulled out of New York harbor on February 1, 1944, and we disembarked in Scotland on February 8.* The zigzag

---

*When specific dates related to events of my personal experiences are cited, my memory is aided by a combination log and documented photo collection, which I compiled during my service time.

crossing for the purpose of evading German submarines was fortunately uneventful. When we first set foot on Scotland, I remember the uncanny experience of seeing there what appeared to be the identical Red Cross women ready to serve hot coffee and doughnuts who had sent us off so cheerily with the same fare as we boarded the Elizabeth in New York. It was equally uncanny that the first tune I heard abroad was "Pistol Packin' Mama," a popular American song of the time.

After more travel by boat, rail, and truck, the four in our cadre wound up in an empty army compound in County Armagh, Northern Ireland. Our duty was to make the place ready, more or less, for the battalion that was to follow. So we were there for two or three weeks before the others came, and this was the most relaxed time I spent until the war was over. It turned out that the place was already in such good order that there was practically nothing to do. We had the Irish to thank for this good fortune.

The Northern Irish turned out to be the most genuinely hospitable people I have ever known, either before or since. This is quite an opinion coming from me because since then I have had experiences with many different peoples in lands all over the world. After the entire battalion had arrived and the villagers became really aware that there were American troops in the compound, they went all out to make us welcome and to make life as pleasant for us as possible. They did have one peculiarity, however: always, without fail, after an introduction to a Northern Irishman, one could predict that his first inquiry would be, "Are you Protestant?" If the answer was yes, his smile broadened and you felt his genuinely unqualified welcome. The people were almost eager to give us the shirts off their backs. I recall how the women would save their sugar rations, which because of the war effort were very small, in order to feed us cakes and tarts at church every Sunday evening after services. In order to do this, many Irish families did without altogether. There was always a big crowd of soldiers to get the sweets because they were the closest we could come to "mama's home cooking" away from home. These people were the most genuinely hospitable I have ever known because they had no expectation or desire for anything in return for their sacrificial interest but to feel that they had made us a little happier. That quality is rare.

Only in the last few years since the open political struggle between the Catholics and Protestants in Northern Ireland have I fully understood what was behind their interest in religious affiliation. At that time, I thought the question mainly reflected their religious piety, not realizing the extreme political significance involved, even though I knew that Southern Ireland was Catholic and neutral during the war. One reason the issue never emerged was that I cannot remember a single man in our outfit who was Catholic. Tony Diego might have been born a Catholic, but he must not have practiced it much, if he was. All the chaplains who served our outfit were Protestant.

However, the most significant point in all this was that as black Americans *we had never before been treated like real human beings by any white people*. The reality of our new situation struck us forcefully when the following incident occurred. This same incident also served to stir up the flames of animosity between the black troops and white officers in our battalion after they had subsided somewhat during the move from the States.

The first Saturday evening after the full battalion had arrived, we noticed a group of officers leave the camp in their dress uniforms for the village hall, which was almost immediately across the street. After about an hour they returned with rather serious expressions on their faces. It turned out that the villagers had sent an invitation to Major McDaniel inviting the battalion to a dance. When about eight or ten of the officers had arrived at the dance, the girls wanted to know where the rest of us were. The officers explained to them, I heard later, that in the United States Army, officers and enlisted men do not fraternize socially; therefore, only the officers had responded to the invitation. Evidently the girls made it clear that eight to ten officers could not quite handle 50 to 60 girls and that they would very much appreciate having more males present for the next dance on the following Saturday. Naturally, we were astounded when we heard this. We had never dreamed of being in a situation where a group of *white girls* would tell Major McDaniel—that stalwart Texas soldier—to his face that they preferred to have a black boy apiece than to share him among themselves!

So the officers reluctantly informed us of the invitation to the dance the following week, and they stayed in camp while we went and had a ball. It was obvious that they resented our socializing with the Irish girls, and they never got used to it. Tension again mounted to a miserable peak, and any excuse they could find to deny a man a pass, they would.

At this point Wakefeld was just about running the battalion because Major McDaniel had become ill and was hospitalized, and our battalion executive officer, who was second in command, was the type who rather happily let an eager beaver like Wakefeld beat his brains out.

One day Wakefeld called a battalion formation to announce that we were going to have a visit from the IG (inspector general). These visits were periodic and for the purpose of determining the current fitness of an outfit to perform its assignment or some new assignment that was in the offing. As part of the inspection, *Army Regulations* provided that any man in an outfit had the privilege of a confidential conference with the IG and would be immune to penalty for it by his superiors. Also, regulations specifically provided that any topic whatsoever could be brought up during such a conference. As I recall, this would be our third visit from an inspector general; the first was when the battalion had failed its basic training, and the second was when we had been given a stamp of approval. Now we guessed that this one was probably for the purpose of determining our readiness to participate in the invasion of the Continent.

Interestingly, I hardly recall that an enlisted man took advantage of this opportunity to complain about conditions in the battalion during the previous IG inspections in the States. Undoubtedly there had been several reasons for this. One was the basic reluctance of most adults to put themselves in the role of a "tattler" if it is at all avoidable. The other was that no one believed that a man who did choose to see the IG would in fact escape Wakefeld's and McDaniel's wrath later. A third and perhaps most important reason was that in those days it was an indelible part of black mentality to have no faith in the concept of "equal protection under the law." We just did not believe that the American "democratic" system (the white man's system) was intended to work for us; rather, we felt that the breaks that came our way, good or bad, were due simply to the whim of the white person or persons who at a particular time had the power to act. An example of this was our joy when Franklin Roosevelt issued the directive, at the beginning of the country's preparations for war, that banned job discrimination in government employment. To some extent this indicated to me that the country needed every resource it could muster, including black labor, *even black trained and educated labor*. But it never crossed my mind that black power, political or otherwise, had had a bit of influence on Roosevelt's action. He was seen primarily as a "benevolent white father." We felt like, acted like, and essentially were at that time a powerless people, and we were convinced that not much could be done to change it.

So when Wakefeld announced another visit by the IG, no one was much surprised. However, what followed topped everything else that had ever come from him or McDaniel. Wakefeld proceeded to order very specifically that anyone requesting to see the IG was forbidden to bring up such topics as pending applications for OCS or ASTP. He went on to stipulate one or two other things we also could not mention that by now I have forgotten. The thing that really shocked me was that I had never thought Wakefeld would openly defy army regulations and do so in a manner suggesting that we would either be too stupid to recognize it, or if we did recognize it we would be too docile to react. The big inspection was about a week away.

I said nothing in the meantime to anyone, but was mulling over whether I felt anything could in fact be gained by my requesting an interview with the IG. I had long since given up the possibility of getting to OCS—since they had not taken me while I was in the States, I hardly thought they would go to the expense of shipping me back to become a "90-day wonder." Naturally I was both disappointed and irritated that I had not been given the chance, because I was fairly certain that there were white guys being accepted whose qualifications were much less than mine. But that was par for the course; and besides, I had been lucky most of my life and had, in fact, become "the first Negro" to do a number of things. Then something developed that entirely changed the course of the situation.

A couple of days later Pfc. Freeman informed me that he was part of a small group of men in the battalion who were trying to organize a 100 percent mass request for interviews with the IG. Their main reason was that not knowing what was in store on the Continent, they simply did not want to undergo whatever it was under the battalion's present leadership. He said they had already obtained a commitment from Master Sergeant Hodge and the two tech sergeants, and now the men wanted to know what my stand would be. He added that he was sure that all the rest of the men would follow if we four top noncoms would go through with it. How interesting! Here again, someone least expected was taking some meaningful initiative, and I was impressed. But I was really no hero and was reluctant to involve myself outrightly in such a conspiracy. I asked Freeman if he was sure of the commitments from Hodge and the other two. He said they had given their word. This from them was difficult to believe indeed. How could it be? I told Freeman that I would have to think it over and that I would let him know in a day or so. He said O.K.

So now my decision making took on much more meaning. The men were trying to do something about a desperate situation, and they were asking us, the top noncoms, to stand up and be counted with them. No inspector general could fail to be impressed if every man in a battalion requested to see him; and if ever there was a chance to get some corrective action, this was it. However, there were also the interim consequences to be considered. If this thing went off even as planned, with every single man going through with it, I was sure there would be some act of retribution as long as Wakefeld and McDaniel drew breath, and especially since McDaniel still did not have his silver leaves. I thought of the personal consequences for me. For what it was worth, I would be putting on the line everything I had accomplished so far in the service, and I knew it. But what was it all worth under these circumstances? Could any other situation be much worse? When I ran my analysis through, I figured that I would have nothing of real significance to lose and would have my self-esteem to gain, and I might be instrumental at the same time in helping a couple of hundred or so other black soldiers gain some of the same. I decided to go through with it. I decided that I would request an interview with the IG whether I was the only man to do so or whether all the men did so. Then I told Freeman of my decision, but I mentioned it to no one else, and no one else mentioned it to me.

The fateful day arrived and Wakefeld called a battalion formation. After a few preliminaries, he announced that the inspector general was available for interviews with anyone wishing to see him, and that all who did wish to see him should take one step forward. There was a moment of hushed silence and no one budged. I hesitated, thinking that maybe Hodge and the two techs might keep their word, but they remained as rigid as stones. I moved one step forward. Then there was the sound of mass movement and every man in the battalion beneath me in rank took one step forward, leaving Hodge and the two techs standing pat. They had done it! The IG was busy interviewing for the rest of the day.

Because of my rank and because I had been the first to step forward, I was the first to be interviewed. Wakefeld had carefully provided a room for the interviews that was just adjacent to his office in a quonset hut, and I knew that the walls were paper thin and that he could hear every word that was being said.

The IG showed obvious concern as well as a very supportive attitude toward what he had just witnessed. He asked my why I had requested to see him, making no reference to the fact that practically the whole battalion was also waiting outside.

I told him that I was gravely concerned for the welfare of the battalion under combat conditions because of a chronic morale problem that had existed from the beginning. He asked for details and I offered as much as I felt I dared since I knew that Wakefeld was listening to every word. Finally he pressed for more specifics and I went so far as to question the adequacy of the battalion's leadership. But when the inspector general asked me to name names, I told him that I did not wish to do so; but rather, I felt that if anyone in authority was really interested, they could conduct an investigation on the basis of the information I had already given.

At this point I was ready to leave, but then the IG asked me about my educational background and work experience. I told him. Then with evident curiosity he asked if I had applied for OCS before leaving the States. I said that I had but had heard nothing from the application. He then directed me to submit another application for OCS immediately; and further, he told me that he would direct my commanding officer to forward the application to SHAEF Headquarters (Supreme Headquarters, Allied Expeditionary Force).

This was certainly an unexpected turn of events, and for once I was glad to believe that Wakefeld was listening because he would know that I had not brought up the subject myself. I eagerly set about completing another OCS application and had it on Wakefeld's desk by the end of the day.

The next day a great calm had settled over everything. There was very little communication between the officers and the enlisted men, and we enlisted men seemed to have less to say to each other. There was little discussion about our mass action. We seemed to have been caught up in an atmosphere of expectancy. Would our action get any results? How would Wakefeld and the officers finally respond? Would there be any reprisals? Because of the apparently sincere concern of the inspector general, I felt less apprehensive about drastic reprisal action; in fact I had begun to feel a great sense of relief.

The day after that, two days after the IG's visit, I was CQ (Charge of Quarters) for the Headquarters Detachment, which meant that I was to be on duty and in charge of the office throughout the night. This was a rotational assignment among the noncommissioned officers in the Detachment, by this time quite routine. Shortly after I came on duty for the evening at about 5:30 P.M., Captain Wakefeld, in his dress uniform, got out of a command car that had driven up in front. The car waited while he came into the headquarters and went back to his office. He emerged in less than five minutes, passed through the outer office and again got into the command car, which drove off in the direction of the main gate.

About 15 minutes later I answered a telephone call from a Colonel Illoson who requested to speak with Captain Wakefeld. I told the colonel that he had just left, but if he would hold on I would try to find out where he had gone and if I could reach him. While the colonel held on, I asked a couple of the men who had been around when Wakefeld came through if he had mentioned where he was going. They seemed to recall his saying something about going to the hospital to visit Major McDaniel, but they were not sure. Nevertheless, all of us had certainly been given the impression that he had driven out of the compound. I conveyed this information to Colonel Illoson who then asked if Lt. Watkins was available. I said that he was, and Illoson dictated a message I was to deliver to him. I wrote down the message, delivered it in person to Lt. Watkins, and proceeded to put the incident out of my mind.

Soon after breakfast the next morning Wakefeld sent for me. He was sitting behind his desk, seemingly unperturbed, and with a matter-of-fact voice he asked if there had been a telephone call for him the previous evening. I said that there had been, but when I had informed Colonel Illoson that he had left the compound, probably to visit Major McDaniel at the hospital, Illoson had directed me to give a message to Lt. Watkins, which I did. Wakefeld then asked how I knew he had left the compound. At that moment I knew something sinister was going on. I explained how I had gotten the impression and what my actions had been. I pointed out specifically that he had been in his dress uniform and had left in a chauffeur-driven command car that was headed for the main gate. He then asked if I had sent a courier to his quarters to check if he was there. I admitted that I had not because under the circumstances I had seen no reason to do so. He then said that was all and dismissed me.

Within hours, Wakefeld issued battalion orders reducing me from staff sergeant to private on the grounds of "inefficiency," and at the same time he informed me that my OCS application would be forwarded to SHAEF Headquarters with an endorsement indicating this action. Further, I was to be transferred out of Battalion Headquarters to a company in the battalion located some distance away. He spelled out all this without batting an eye.

I was practically limp. He had really done a complete job of reducing me, army-wise, to zero. He had even delayed forwarding my OCS application until he could complete his scheme. I had to admit that his performance had caught me quite off guard and surpassed even my wildest expectations, especially in terms of the grounds that he had concocted—probably with help. Then to top it off, he kicked me out of headquarters but still kept control over me! Obviously he did not feel it would ever be necessary for him to explain how a man he had previously given only excellent efficiency ratings had suddenly become so grossly inefficient.

It is impossible to describe the excrutiating mixture of emotions all this brought on. I was frightened, angry, depressed, and frustrated; but at the same time this action made me feel all the more justified by what I had done and the way in which I had done it. Now I felt most threatened by the knowledge that I was still at the mercy of a couple of men who finally revealed themselves to have no scruples and seemingly no conscience. The only thing I had gained was a little distance between them and me.

A great sense of defeat hung over all the men, and an attitude of resignation set in. My one regret was leaving them feeling that perhaps nothing had been accomplished after all. Because Wakefeld was convinced that I had instigated this protest action, he succeeded in making me a martyr and hero in their eyes. I was happy that he did not know the truth and that he would still have to contend with strengths in his men that he refused to recognize.

As the jeep carried me off with the faded impressions of my former four stripes on each arm, I shall never forget the crowd of men as they stood around with their good-byes and Diego and Freeman waving with tears in their eyes.

My principal job in Battalion Headquarters had been Personnel Sergeant Major. My embarrassment was increased by the fact that the company to which I was being transferred was one I had visited only a couple of weeks before for the purpose of inspecting their personnel records. Lt. Aimes, my new company commander, called me into his office right away to lay down the law and to let me know exactly where I stood. He said he had been told by Wakefeld that I was one of those smart college-trained Negroes (he meant niggers) who had been an agitator ever since I had been in the service, and he wanted me to know that he would stand for none of that in his company. He wanted me to know that he was the commander of this company and nobody was going to take over the command from him, and most certainly not one of his enlisted men. Aimes seemed to be threatened by my presence.

I wondered just how much more I could take. Here was a man reaming me out on first sight and already convinced that I would constitute a danger in his company from what Wakefeld had told him. With every ounce of fortitude I could muster, I managed to contain myself and to have the presence of mind to say to Lt. Aimes that I would make just one request of him, which was that he form his opinion of me as a result of his own experiences with me and not as a result of something he had heard, especially if it came from Wakefeld. I was surprised and somewhat relieved when he quite frankly replied that he would be glad to do that. Then he turned me over to his top sergeant.

I had met Jones, his top sergeant, during my previous inspection trip. When we were alone, he told me how sorry he was to learn of my trouble and he reassured me that eventually everything would be all right for me here. It would just take a little time. However, it was his unpleasant task to give me my duty assignments, which had been ordered by Battalion Headquarters: every other day I was to clean the company latrines, and on all other days I was to walk guard duty. That was all.

So this was Wakefeld's final trick. He was treating me as though I had been tried by a courtmartial and sentenced to hard labor; and if I rebelled or refused to do as I was told, he would then have his excuse to haul me before a courtmartial for disobeying a direct order and have me sent to the stockade.

It so happened that I knew something about Aimes' relationship with Wakefeld, which could be quite an asset in our coming to terms with each other. I knew that basically Aimes was not a bad guy and that he was still a first lieutenant commanding his company overseas when rightfully he should have been promoted to captain some time ago. His promotion was being held up in Battalion Headquarters (which meant by Wakefeld) because Aimes' men were notorious for looking sloppy in their uniforms, and Wakefeld felt that Aimes did not show sufficient concern about this. One of the main bones of contention was Aimes' company clerk, Cpl. Rich, who, though he was a very efficient company clerk, simply refused to wear the proper headgear. It seemed that Wakefeld particularly delighted in catching Rich on pass outside the army compound in an "improper uniform." He would call Lt. Aimes and report Rich, and then order Aimes to mete out the "proper punishment" and to impose pass restrictions. It seems that Aimes' punishment never quite satisfied Wakefeld; and too often when Wakefeld thought Rich should be on restriction, he would be out with a proper pass, though improperly dressed. So Aimes and I were really in somewhat the same position vis-á-vis our Captain Wakefeld.

Therefore, without one word of objection I cleaned the

latrines to perfection and walked guard duty as if on display in front of Buckingham Palace. This went on for about two weeks and I still uttered not one complaint, nor did I look to the right or to the left while walking my post. I realized that Aimes was scrutinizing me from a distance, at first in puzzled disbelief. Certainly this could not be "the smart nigger agitator" from headquarters—he had never had such clean latrines, nor had he ever had a man in his company who dressed so well and walked guard duty in such a military manner.

One day Lt. Aimes came up and addressed me while I was on guard. I halted, saluted and stood at attention. He said "O.K., O.K., at ease." I could tell by the tone of his voice and his manner that I had won. I felt very good inside. He said that he had an opening in one of his platoons for a corporal and wondered if I would be interested. I said that I sure would. Then, apologetically, he went on to say that as company commander he could issue orders himself making me a pfc., but I would have to wait for corporal's stripes until the day his company might not be under our present battalion command, because he knew that "they" would never approve my promotion as "they" would have to do. I told him that I understood quite well the position he was in and thanked him for his confidence in me. I felt he got my double message.

In a week or so our company was moved from Ireland to Swindon, England, where we bivouacked for several weeks. During the move our company was fortunately separated from the old battalion and reassigned. In a few days Aimes had his double captain's bars and I had my two corporal's stripes. There was such great activity all over that we knew the time for the invasion was drawing near and the suspense was killing. Buzz bombs had begun to drop on London, and I was lucky to have had one 24-hour pass there just the day before the first one fell. After that, all passes to London were canceled.

I had been assigned as one of a group from our company to get training in the use of the 50-calibre machine gun. We had been converted into a quartermaster truck company and these machine guns would be mounted on every fourth vehicle. So we set out from Swindon early one morning for the day-long truck ride to the machine gun range on the coast of the North Sea. The highways were clogged and there were all kinds of traffic delays. It was June 4, 1944, and quite warm for that season of the year. By the time we arrived at the British army camp where we were to stay, it was dark, and there was still considerable delay before we could learn from anyone in authority just where we were to bed down. Finally we were shown to a large army barracks, which looked as if it had not been used in years. Dust was an inch thick over everything including the lumpy, hard mattresses. The floor was grimy and littered with trash. Cobwebs were everywhere. Well, in the service, this means only one thing: a thorough cleanup, making the cots, and proper arrangement of gear before any rest and sleep. So we got to it, because the sooner it was done the sooner we could flop. After about two hours of steady labor the place had been made quite decent. Our officer in charge had come in and made bed check and left.

But a few minutes later he returned in the company of a British officer who announced that, regretfully, a mistake had been made, that this was not the barracks we were to stay in, and that we would have to relocate immediately. Had it not been for sheer military discipline the place would have gone up for grabs. We pleaded to know why we had to move after working like dogs to clean up that filthy hole. But sorry, chaps, there had been an error; we would simply have to move. Our officer was obviously disturbed by it all but told us that he had no authority in the matter since we were guests in effect. So we got our gear together and straggled out into the night.

We were led to another barracks about a block away. The British officer said that this was it—this was where we were to stay, and good night. When we entered this place it was unbelievable. Could it really be in worse condition than the first one had been? It was, and we had to go to it all over again. It seemed our torture would never end!

Our officer hung around a minute or so to see that the work got under way. He was uneasy and apologetic, and his random comments were an attempt at throw off, like "this is the army," and that sort of crap. Then someone confronted him with: "Lieutenant, why don't you tell us the reason for all this?" Then he said something about these camps being set up in a certain way, and somebody just made a mistake, that's all, someone had goofed and, well, somebody had directed us to a barracks in the *white section!* He wished us good night and left.

All the next day we black men gripped those 50-calibre guns with a vengeance, sending tracers and incendiaries toward a target sleeve dragged by a plane at the end of a long line. Out they arched over the North Sea draining away our anger. At a still further distance, beyond our range, boats ploughed back and forth—boats of all sizes and descriptions, going, moving about in crazy senseless patterns

—boats too numerous to count, an unimaginable armada. Something was surely about to happen.

All day long, the sound of the guns and the movement of the boats were a kind of rhythmical background for words that forced themselves into my mind—thoughts and verse that insisted on being born.

> My soul from out the gloom of bondage cries
> Some sense of unknown freedom to be sought
> As one who stares from out his cell of bars
> At paradise unbounded—him denied
>
> Born as it was within this ghettoed world
> Paled as is grass with dirth of sun
> Roots strain and pierce the fertile soil of thought
> But few the buds of flavored fruit can bear
>
> My soul would quit this dank and narrow cell
> And venture forth upon the green expanse!
> For in a dream it thought a hand of white
> Did wave and beckon welcome from afar
>
> Through bar and out as specter would it went
> To travel length and breadth and over seas
> And in each land it gave and shared its all
> To make the paradise of green more green
>
> But as each day would end and sun would set
> And after toil and sweat it sought repose
> Instead of couch of green beneath the stars
> The reaper of the labor gave—a cell
>
> So soon my soul now crushed and scourged did learn
> The pale dream hand a vampire nature had!
> Thus if a cell was all it had to gain
> Of all the cells it did prefer its own
>
> Awake from dreams it now must contemplate
> The bitter wisdom that the vision gave—
> If paradise there was it was not this
> Nor yet a home nor peace nor understanding.

This projection of my intense feelings into words is identified in my personal papers by a note, as follows:

> Written in England, on the coast of the North Sea, 5 June 1944, while filled with dejection because of a deliberate and gross incident of racial segregation on the part of the American and British military forces which forced undue discomfort in living conditions on a group of American Negro soldiers, particularly of the 4050th QM Trk Co, Third U. S. Army.

The next day the Allied forces stormed Fortress Europa.

It was D day plus 34, the 10th of July, 1944, when our company landed on Omaha Beachhead. Our bivouac area was just outside Bricquebec in Normandy, France. For what seemed to be endless days we had nothing to do but to keep ourselves in readiness for the big push when we would break out of the beachhead and start the bloody trek across France. At night the inevitable German planes came at high risk to drop their bombs amid arching fountains of ack-ack that recalled all Fourth of Julys. Each morning we were grateful that one more night had been survived.

Then finally, early on the evening of July 31, Captain Aimes called his noncoms together for a crucial briefing. The 4050th Quartermaster Truck Company had been chosen to become a rolling ammunition supply source for Third Army field artillery. We were to move out immediately. When *Patton's Wheels* (Davis, 1945) was published at the end of the European war, it contained the following comment about our assignment:

> In the middle of one very dark night late in July, the 4050th QM Truck Company was dispatched from the Bricquebec area to report to VIII Corps. The sergeant making out the required dispatch for the trip was handing out just one more routine QM truck assignment. But the 4050th didn't return from the routine assignment for nearly three weeks during which time it served as a rolling ammunition reserve in support of the VIII Corps units which were running wild into the Brittany Peninsula.
>
> The Peninsula campaign was the first of many operations to weld a strong bond of fighting friendship between the tankers, the doughfeet, and the QM truck drivers [p. 3].

In our sector of the beachhead, the breakthrough was in the St. Lo-Coutances area. For 17 days and nights without a break our trucks ground over pockmarked roads with loads of ammo from the communication zone, moving it up to feed the big guns. The front ran forward relentlessly under the Third Army's thrust, lengthening our supply lines and our round-trip distance. Seventeen days and nights—eat as catch can, sleep as catch can, and never a moment even to change our clothes. Granville, Avranches, Laval, Le Mans, Chartres—the list of familiar places along our route grew longer each day.

France was crossed and for a while the pace slackened. But then during the last of December and through January there was the Ardennes Campaign, or the Battle of the Bulge, described as "...without doubt the most concentrated and bloodiest operation of the Third US Army during the European War [G-3 Historical Sub-Section, 1945]." By the time that had been survived, the winter had become cruel. We were happy to settle in a small village in Luxembourg called Hautcharage in order to collect ourselves before entering Germany. We crossed the Rhine in March, and by this time I had gained another stripe and was a sergeant.

Lt. Colonel Hathaway, a southern gentleman from Virginia turned army officer, was in command of our battalion. One day he sent for me and my reaction was "Oh, God—not again!" He informed me that SHAEF Headquarters was going to award a number of battlefield commissions, making men second lieutenants directly without their having to go to OCS, and he had recommended me for one. I would first have to go before a reviewing board for an evaluation, but he suggested it would be rather routine. I thanked him for his consideration but regretfully informed him that it probably would not be so routine with me, and I asked him if he had ever looked at my service record. He said no, and wondered why I asked. I told him that I had once been reduced from staff sergeant to private for "inefficiency," and it was very plainly recorded in my service record. Hathaway, shocked, asked something like what kind of garbage was I trying to give him. I told him it was the truth and when he had about an hour to spare sometime, I would be glad to fill him in. He said he had an hour "right now!" and I began my tale. When I was finished, I told him again how much I appreciated his nomination, and that I was sorry that I could not be a candidate for a direct commission from his outfit. He retorted with, "Why not?" He resolved to send me to the board anyway, and he told me that if they asked about the service record entry, I was to explain it to them just as I had explained it to him. They asked, and I explained.

On April 13, 1945, the day we heard that President Roosevelt was dead, I was made a second lieutenant in Alsfeld, Germany.

There had been a company formation and a brief ceremony, which had ended just before lunch. Instantly, my life changed. I was escorted to a dining room in a nearby building, which was the officers' mess. We sat down to white tablecloths and napkins and glistening plates and flatware. I had seated myself by a window. The sun was shining brightly and the day was warm. The window looked out over the enlisted men's mess line. Moving in a long queue, after they got their food slapped in their mess kits, they sat on the ground to eat. They were so accustomed to the swirls of dust that seasoned their meal each time a vehicle passed that they hardly noticed. There they were out there—those great guys with whom I had shared and experienced so much.

I thought of Diego and Freeman and Morse and all my buddies back in the old battalion. I wondered where they were now and how well they had continued to survive the two fronts of the black soldier: the domestic as well as the foreign. Rumor had it that McDaniel never made it across the Channel, and that Wakefeld had made major. I looked around the room at all the white faces and the glistening officers' insignia. Outside the window the black soldiers were eating in the dust. I looked at the food-laden plate in front of me. *Where did I belong?* I felt empty and dazed and could not eat.

References

Davis, S. M. (Ed.) *Patton's wheels*. European Theater of Operations: Expeditionary Force Field Press, 1945.

G-3 Historical Sub-Section. *Third Army, a brief history of operations in Europe*. European Theater of Operations: Allied Expeditionary Force Field Press, 1945.

Epilogue

We have come over a way that with tears has been watered,
We have come, treading our path through the blood of the slaughtered,
Out from the gloomy past,
Till now we stand at last
Where the white gleam of our bright star is cast ...
[From "Lift Ev'ry Voice and Sing" by J. W. Johnson.
©Copyright Edward B. Marks Music Corporation. Used by permission.]

Chapter Seven
Black Psychological Survival

An 11-year-old predicts dauntlessly to a white schoolmate that his life will be richer because of the struggle due to his blackness in a white racist society. But that 11-year-old, grown to advanced adulthood after the fact of much of that struggle, though enriched is now amazed that the residual scars are not deeper and more pervasive. As a psychologist he finds it "inexplicable" that emotional disorders among blacks have no greater incidence than they do, that blacks have shunned communism, have fought in ridiculous wars, and have remained loyal to this country despite the nature of the black experience.

"Where do I belong?" is the disquieting quandary felt in 1945 by a young black lieutenant converted "in the twinkling of an eye" from enlisted man to officer as he sits strangely among white officers in the comfort of their mess, watching his black brothers outside eating on the ground. Thus his longed-for achievement precipitated a quandary of affiliation—a kind of state of separation from his own —which, especially in the past, was often the situation for the black person who attained some novel success.

Who am I really, and what is my worth as a human being? Where do I belong? Where is my rightful allegiance? Such are the identity issues and states of being that have been generated in the black American by the peculiar and many-faceted nature of the American black experience. The autobiographical excerpts from the lives of two black psychologists in Part III are reflections from just a few of those facets and serve to illustrate some of the ways the issues that are the concerns of Parts I and II of this book are generated.

What of "Black Psychology"?

Is there a black psychology? And if so, what are its principles? The involvement of some black undergraduate psychology students with this question gained sufficient prominence at one point that it was given attention in the press (Student Psychologists, 1970). Caught up in the fervor of black consciousness, it seemed that those students were eager to find grounds for a complete uniqueness of blackness —quite a turnabout from the late 40s and early 50s when it seemed that the prime interest of many blacks, as well as some white liberals, was to rationalize "no difference" between whites and blacks.

Psychology as a scientific discipline attempts to discover universal principles of human psychological functioning, learning, and experiencing on the assumption that such universals do exist, elusive though they may be. The countless frustrations encountered in psychological research and in the pursuit of more useful conceptual models have not yet led to a rejection of this basic assumption of universal principles of behavior that apply to the human species across the board. Greater care is now exercised in the designation of "universals" than in the past, however, and the pitfalls that led to false identifications as well as some of the gross errors that were made in this regard are now recognized. A classical example was the Oedipus complex of psychoanalysis, which Fanon (1967, pp. 151–152) and many others have exposed to be invalid as a universal development. A major fact of psychological observation is that the conditions and combinations of factors that can impinge on and affect behavior are countless. Thus there are many instances of atypical behavioral products that result from the unique conditions in which growth and behavior have taken place. For example, child development may have different outcomes from one culture to another, but the basic principles of interpersonal learning are assumed to be the same.

Just as there is yet insufficient evidence to reject the basic assumption of universal principles of behavior that operate from one human group to another, there is considerable evidence for the assumption that the conditions which have impinged on American blacks from the beginning of their history in this country have been psychologically quite singular and have, therefore, produced in American blacks as a people certain behavioral products that are essentially unique in human history. As presented in Part I, these are (a) a generalized conflict in self-esteem associated with adaptive inferiority, (b) anxiety being conditioned to one's color of skin, and (c) anxiety over intellectual assertion and competition. The importation of Africans as slaves to this country constitutes the greatest known mass manipulation of human beings for the purpose of molding their behavior to comply with predetermined criteria. Therefore, in another sense, the history of the Afro-American has constituted the greatest social-psychological "experiment" of all time, when the conditions of the experiment were not in whole or in part self-imposed.

There is then no *black psychology* that embodies its own distinctive set of psychological principles; but there is quite legitimately a *psychology of the black experience,* which is the study of the special conditions of Afro-American history and the psychological effects that have been specific to those conditions.

Principles for Black Psychological Survival

The following are five broad-based statements deemed minimally essential for the continued psychological survival and self-actualization of black Americans. These same principles might also serve as nuclear concepts for a contemporary social science of the black experience.

First: Effective consolidation of the national black community must be achieved through education for the recognition of common goals and purposes, which can be pursued successfully only through the unification of identity, the neutralization of class boundaries, and the strengthening of communication, understanding, and cooperation at all levels.

Continuing efforts toward achieving a more effective unification of the national black community is of first-order importance. Progress in this direction will have an ongoing relationship with the further resolution of conflict in the area of individual self-esteem and the enlargement of mutual respect and appreciation throughout the black population. The serious problems that still exist in this regard cannot be minimized, and the reality is that time itself will be an important factor in the eventual solution of these problems. There is still an unfortunate lack of basic rapport and trust between the majority of American blacks and that smaller segment referred to as the "black middle class." Fortunately, however, the magnitude of this schism is now largely correlated with the age of the individuals. This problem will be progressively minimized with the growing to maturity of the black youth of today who recognize the disadvantages of such a schism and who reject the false values on which such class divisions are based. Let it be remembered, however—in defense of many members of the so-called "black middle class"—that they came along in a different day when for the black person almost any accomplishment in this society was obtained on a go-it-alone basis and on the terms of the white power structure or not at all; that the validity of their achievements or their competence after years of struggle was often least appreciated by their own people; and that, above all, their accomplishments were often a sort of pioneering that resulted in a state of alienation in which they were neither understood nor fully trusted by their own nor given the recognition they deserved by the white majority. The black bourgeoisie in America today are no less the victims of white racism than are the less privileged masses, their greater material comfort notwithstanding.

> *Second:* There must be an ongoing assessment and implementation of a philosophy and strategy of existence as a black minority among a white majority in the United States based on the realities of constant change in culture, social relationships, educational necessities, politics, economics, and international power positions.
>
> *Third:* The principle must be recognized that short- and long-range programs directed toward the immediate relief of social problems and the negative conditions of blacks can best be devised and administered by blacks.

The second and third priorities imply that the black minority in this country can no longer, for its own good, risk a nonplanned existence; and that following a planned existence as a minority and the assumption of responsibility for its own welfare are consonant with the central purposes of the Black Revolution and the rejection of a controlling dependency relationship to the overall society.

> *Fourth:* There must be the realization that the ills of the black minority, an 11 percent of the whole U. S. population, reflect and are intrinsically related to the ills of the total society, and that their ultimate rectification as social ills is not separable.

In my opinion, the inability to realize and accept this fourth concept is the most serious failing of contemporary American society as a whole and its governing structures from federal to municipal. One could venture that if violent revolution ever does come to pass again in this country, it will be between those who are painfully aware of this relationship and assign it the highest priority and those who are blind to it, regardless of racial, religious, or other identities.

> *Fifth:* The enhancement of relationships with blacks of the African continent must be an ongoing policy, and every support must be given to their achieving full freedom as people and as a collection of cooperating governments.

It is inconceivable that American blacks could seek their own freedom and be unconcerned about the still existing states of colonialism and oppression of black peoples in other parts of the world. The situations of obvious oppression of blacks in Africa are easily recognized and are all too well-known. Not so well known are the states of economic oppression and economic colonialism that characterize the conditions of the people of many so-called independent countries of Africa.

It is not at all difficult for the average American black to empathize with the man-without-a-country feeling, and the older he is the easier this is to do. Like other peoples of the world, American blacks have longed for the feeling of truly belonging to a country—to a piece of this earth—and in that search have turned increasingly to the west coast of Africa, the land of our forefathers. The return affords an interesting experience—at long last, to stand on the earth that gave birth to one's ancestors. The recognition of kinship with the people is inescapable, but the comfortable feeling of belonging is not there. It could come perhaps with time, but there is an irrational disappointment that it is not immediate. On visiting Africa, one realizes that the present-day American black is a distinctive melding of bloods, cultures, and experiences, and that now his legitimate home is the place that gave birth to that melding. But the kinship with African peoples remains, and rapport will build on that kinship increasingly with time. On visiting Africa, one is left feeling that this is truly the continent of the future.

This series of essays and autobiographical accounts began with the observation that the Black Revolution is born out of the American black man's will for survival, his will to surmount the effects of radical oppression, and his will toward self-actualization. The uniqueness of the black American's accomplishments is supported by the extraordinary historical circumstances in which they were achieved. It was no accident that the opening emphasis here was on the American black man's strengths; for in any objective sense, his strengths have always been his most impressive though often least-credited attributes.

References

Fanon, F. *Black skin, white masks*. New York: Grove Press, 1967.
Johnson, J. W. Lift every voice and sing. In L. Hughes and A. Bontemps (Eds.), *The poetry of the Negro, 1946–1949*. Garden City, N. Y.: Doubleday & Co., 1949, 32–33.
Student psychologists plot action at Chicago conference. *Jet,* 1970, **39** (Dec. 17), 24–25.

Glossary

This glossary is intended to make this volume more useful for persons who have little familiarity with the technical terminology of psychology. The definitions are, therefore, as succinct as possible and often relate to the specific context in which the words, terms, or concepts are used.

Ack-ack. Fire from antiaircraft guns, in this instance consisting of visible tracer bullets.
Activism, activists. See p. 27.
Act-out. The expression of an unconscious conflict or impulse in outward behavior or actions.
Adaptive inferiority. See p. 12.
Adjustment, psychological. A dynamic process, largely learned through experience, that characterizes how a person copes with experience. The word does not imply passive compliance, although passive compliance is a type of adjustment pattern.
Ambivalent. Having at the same time different and opposing feelings or notions about something.
Anxiety. Emotional discomfort similar to uneasiness, apprehension, and dread combined. Anxiety accompanies extreme stress, frustration, or unconscious conflict.
Anxiety state. An emotional reaction in which anxiety is a dominant feature.

Assessment, objective. Measurement or evaluation of attitudes, personality attributes, or behavior with the use of questionnaires or psychological tests.

Behavior modification. A method of changing behavior (a therapy) that systematically uses learning theory and reinforcements such as rewards and punishments.

Bivouac area. A location for pitching tents and setting up a military camp.

Bourgeois; black bourgeoisie. "Middle class" as opposed to "lower class." In black society a difference determined by greater education, income, or a white-collar family background. Currently the term carries negative implications because of the need on the part of some bourgeois blacks to hold themselves apart from the black masses.

Brain impulse tendency. This refers to the pattern of electrical energy that is related to the functioning of the brain. The graphical representation of "brain waves" is called the electroencephalogram (EEG).

Change agent. A person who acts to change social conditions.

Chemotherapy. The use of drugs for changing or controlling behavior, including feelings or thought processes. Often used concurrently with psychotherapy.

Conceptual mode. An explanation; an idea or projection of the structure, organization, nature, or purpose of something that may or may not have proven validity. If unproven, it serves a theoretical purpose until its validity can be established or a better model can be devised.

Conditioned; conditioning. Conditioning is a type of learning process. In many instances it may involve a type of learning that would not have occurred under ordinary circumstances; e.g., the particular social experiences of American blacks have caused them to develop anxiety about their skin color, something that would not have occurred in a society free of racism.

Conflict; inner conflict. The state of one need or drive being opposed to another or being otherwise frustrated. Part or all of this process is usually at an unconscious level of experience.

Congruence; congruence of self. See p. 12.

Conscious. A state of awareness; having immediate knowledge of experience. See *Unconscious*.

Control work. That part of psychoanalytic training in which the student carries out the analysis of a patient under the supervision of a training analyst.

Controlled investigation. An investigation carried out according to scientific method in order to insure the greatest certainty regarding findings and conclusions.

Conversion symptoms. A physical symptom that has no apparent physical cause and is assumed to have an emotional basis.

Corrective emotional learning. See *Corrective experience*.

Corrective experience. An experience that promotes the learning of feelings, attitudes, and behaviors that contribute to more effective adjustment and functioning.

Countertransference. In psychotherapy or psychoanalysis, the need on the part of the therapist to behave toward the client in ways that were learned in the therapist's past relationships but which are not appropriate for his relationship with the client. See *Transference*.

Defense; defensive mechanism. In psychodynamic theory, a behavior development or other symptom that is the more recognizable evidence of an underlying psychological conflict and that serves to reduce the anxiety which that conflict produces. See *Denial*.

Denial. A psychological defense that helps a person to control anxiety by his refusing to recognize or admit to the experience that produces it.

Dependent measures. In a scientific experiment, that which is supposed to change as a result of altering some other condition (an independent measure).

Depressive reaction. A state of dejection and sadness that seriously interferes with one's ability to function.

Determinism; deterministic. From philosophy, the theory that everything that occurs within natural events and human behavior has been caused by something else.

Diagnosis. An evaluation of the nature of a behavior disorder or adjustment problem. A classification or description.

Didactic analysis. The part of psychoanalytic training that is the personal analysis of the student in training.

Doughfeet. World War II slang term for infantry.

Drug therapy. See *Chemotherapy*.

Dynamic-experiential. Referring to the interrelationship of the many processes involved in the realization of experience.

Dynamics; psychodynamics. The interaction between the various components of personality, behavior, and psychological functioning.

Ego. From psychoanalytic theory, in simplest terms, the central capacity of the individual for organizing a self-system and an approach to the management of experiences. Ego, id, and superego are interrelated concepts.

Ego-ideal. The idea a person has of what he would like to be.

En masse (French). In very large numbers.

Ethics. A generally accepted standard of conduct in relationships between persons of a particular group, society, or culture.

Ethnocentric. Race-centered or culture-centered.

Etiology. Causes; the process by which something comes about or develops.

Experimenter effect. In a scientific experiment or investigation, some influence on the results, usually unintended, caused by certain characteristics of the person carrying out the experiment.

Experimenter variable. Something about the experimenter (such as age, sex, or race) that might influence the outcome of the experiment.

Feedback. In interpersonal relationships, reactions to or opinions about a person's behavior or personality characteristics that are conveyed to him by others.

Frame of reference. A point of view. More specifically, a particular way of looking at or examining a set of circumstances that allows one to find meaning in them.

Fröhliche Weihnacht und glückliches neues Jahr (German). Merry Christmas and Happy New Year.

Genetic-constitutional. Pertaining to inherited factors over which the individual has no control.

Hypnotherapy. The use of hypnosis in psychotherapy or for the purpose of controlling or changing behavior or adjustment.

Hypothesis. An assumption, often a part of a theory, that may be tested by experimentation.

Glossary

Identification with the aggressor. A defense mechanism, such as for purposes of self-protection; an oppressed person's accepting the thinking and actions of his oppressor as being justified, rather than risking assertion against the oppressor.

Identity; identification. A set of characteristics that distinguish one person or group from another.

Incorporated. In psychodynamic theory, adopted, taken into, or made a part of the self. See *Introjection.*

Industrialization. The development of mass production of goods and produce.

Insight. An understanding or comprehension, generally at an intellectual level, of oneself or of some psychological problem.

Institutionalized authoritarianism. Strict obedience to authority as a standard expectation of an organization or society.

Instructional set. The inclination to respond in a way that has been determined by the instructions given for a task.

Integration; reintegration. In psychodynamic terms, organizing or reorganizing the patterns of one's behavior or adjustment.

Intrapsychic. Inner or subjective processes of personality or the self-system, usually at the unconscious level.

Introjection. Taking into or making something a part of oneself. See *Incorporated.*

Liberal; liberal movement. Opposed to conservative. Inclined toward change rather than clinging to tradition and the status quo.

Libido. From classical psychoanalytic theory, the concept of instinctual and/or sexual energy as a central factor of intrapsychic dynamics. Revisions of psychoanalytic theory, or the neo-analytic positions, reject the concept of libido.

Masochism; masochistic. Broadly speaking, the management of life's experiences so that, in the long run, one is habitually hurt or put to a disadvantage.

Mess. The place where the military is served meals; the meal itself.

Minority paranoia. A chronic suspiciousness and distrust toward the majority in a society on the part of some smaller group as a result of the smaller group's negative experience with the majority.

Motivation. The matter of being moved to act, to behave, or to accomplish something.

Narcissistic. The love of self in the extreme as contrasted with appropriate self-esteem.

Oedipus complex; oedipal competition. From psychoanalytic theory, pertaining to a son's over-attachment to his mother along with his need to compete with or replace the father in the mother's affections.

Oedipal material. Behavior or fantasies related to the Oedipus complex.

Oedipal transference. The reaction of a patient toward the therapist in psychoanalysis or psychotherapy as the patient reacted toward the parent during his "oedipal stage" of development.

Oral. In psychoanalysis, the first stage of psychosexual development. Refers to the overwhelming importance of eating and taking things into the mouth. Oral needs are related to dependency, and when one is "oral demanding" he aggressively insists on being taken care of.

Parameter. Loosely, as now often used, the delimiting characteristics of something.

Participatory democracy. Having power retained by the people and exercised through their joint action.
Personality. The dynamic manifestations of thinking, behavior, and adjustment that give each individual a uniqueness.
Phallic-sadistic. In simplest terms, having both masculine and punitive qualities.
Polarize. To become separated into different, often opposing, positions or factions.
Politicized. To make politically aware, and therefore to have one's actions influenced by political goals.
Prognosis. An estimation of the future course of a behavior disorder or some other process.
Psychodrama. The use of role-acting in psychotherapy.
Psychoanalysis; psychoanalytic. The comprehensive, systematic theory of human behavior originated by Sigmund Freud. Also the method for correcting personality disturbances based on that theory. A form of psychotherapy.
Psychodiagnostic. Pertaining to methods such as psychological tests or interviewing that are used to determine a person's pattern of behaving and adjusting.
Psychological defense. See *Defense*.
Psychology; psychological. The scientific study of human and animal behavior.
Psychopathology. Most common usage: maladaptive behavior patterns.
Psychosexual. In psychoanalysis, personal growth and development is divided into psychosexual stages that represent levels of personal and sexual maturity.
Psychosis. A more severe disorder of adjustment and psychological functioning than a neurosis, for example, and accompanied by bizarre behavior.
Psychosocial. Pertaining to both psychological and social aspects of experience.
Psychotherapy; psychotherapeutic interaction. The relationship between client and therapist in which the client learns new and more effective ways of behaving, relating to others, and coping with experience. See *Psychoanalysis*.
Psychotherapy, dynamic individual. The one-to-one psychotherapeutic relationship. See *Psychotherapy*.
Psychotherapy, group. The use of the small group and its more numerous relationship possibilities for purposes of psychotherapy. See *Psychotherapy*.
Quartermaster Corps. That branch of the army concerned with supplies.
Radical; radicalized. One who advocates immediate and revolutionary changes in laws, methods of government, and social relationships, for example.
Rapport. Good feeling between people that allows them to relate and cooperate effectively.
Reaction; reaction pattern. A way of behaving or a set of behaviors that is in response to some experience.
Reaction formation. Overt behavior that is opposite to unconscious need. This is a psychological defense.
Reinforcement conditions. Circumstances under which reward or punishment is given.
Repress; repression. From psychoanalytic theory, the process of keeping certain disturbing thoughts or feelings out of conscious awareness.
Resistance; resistances. In psychotherapy, evidence of the client's unwilling-

ness or unreadiness to accomplish certain corrective learnings or to give up certain defenses.

Response tendencies. Usual or predictable ways of acting in certain situations or under particular conditions.

Role playing. See *Psychodrama.*

Schizophrenia; schizophrenic. The most common diagnosis among the psychotic disorders.

Schizophrenic reaction, paranoid type. The common type of schizophrenia, dominated by irrational fear of harm from others, or sometimes by irrational ideas of one's own powers.

Self-actualize; self-actualization. The matter of becoming a complete person and developing all of one's potentialities.

Self-concept. What a person thinks he is; how one visualizes oneself.

Self-esteem. The value one puts on oneself—the central aspect of self-concept.

Self-fulfilling prophecy. A prediction that comes true because people have been led to expect it and behave according to their expectations, thus producing that which was predicted.

Self-system. From H. Sullivan's interpersonal theory, in simplest terms, what one has learned to think of or to mean when he refers to "I," "me," or "my."

Sensitivity training. Learning to understand oneself better and to relate to others more effectively through participating in a small laboratory group conducted by a facilitator or trainer.

Sibling rivalry. Competition among brothers and sisters.

Somatic delusion. An illogical, false belief about the condition of one's body.

Stereotype; stereotypic. A preconceived notion about the members of a particular group.

Superego. From psychoanalysis, in simplest terms, that part of personality organization that is conscience, or feelings about right and wrong.

Supportive therapies. Efforts that emphasize encouragement and guidance toward helping a person to function at his best.

Symbiotic. A type of overdependent relationship between people who are unable to function without each other.

Syndrome. A particular pattern of behaviors or reactions that characterize a condition of adjustment.

Taboo. An avoidance of something dictated by social custom and supported by fear of the consequences if violated.

Task content. That which a participant (subject) in an experiment is required to do.

Transference. In psychotherapy or psychoanalysis, the need on the part of the client to behave toward the therapist in ways that were learned in a past relationship but that are not appropriate for the present.

Transference, hostile. When the transference reaction is also characterized by hostile-aggressive feelings. See *Transference.*

Traumatic. Very harmful or disruptive, sometimes with lasting effects.

Umlaut. In German, a mark(¨) placed over a vowel that changes the way it is pronounced.

Unconscious. Originally a psychoanalytic concept. A level of inner experience and need of which one is not aware but that nevertheless influences outward behavior and adjustment.

Variable. Something that can be measured and that can have different numerical values under differing conditions (for example, age, heart rate, or intelligence quotient).

Victory, Costa Rica. The Costa Rica was one of many so-called "Victory Ships" that were mass-produced during World War II.

Western civilization. The culture, society, institutions, and customs of Europe and America.

Name Index

Adams, W. A., 39, 42, 43, 52
Anderson, E. "Rochester," 15
Aquinas, T., 59
Aristotle, 59
Armstrong, H., 15
Babcock, C. G., 40, 52
Bay, C., 27, 34
Bender, L., 40, 52
Bennett, L., 9, 11, 20, 24
Bloombaum, M., 41, 53
Bontemps, A., 24, 108
Calnek, M., 41, 43, 49, 50, 52
Carmichael, S., 4, 8, 24
Chrisman, R., 4, 24
Cobbs, P., 11, 39, 42, 52
Crowley, M. R., 14, 24
Curry, A., 39, 42, 45, 46, 47, 48, 49, 52
Davis, S. M., 97, 99
Davis, T. E., 14, 24
Doob, L. W., 40, 51, 52
Douglass, F., 9
DuBois, W. E. B., 11
Edwards, T. J., v, vi, viii, 17, 65–72
Eisenhower, D. D., 7
Evers, M., 8
Fanon, F., 104, 108
Frank, J. D., 39, 41, 43, 52
Frazier, E. F., 14, 24
Freud, S., 59
G-3 Historical Sub-Section, 98, 99

Gandy, J. M., 14, 24
Gardner, L. H., v, vi, viii, 37–53
Greenson, R. R., 44, 52
Gregg, H. D., 14, 24
Grier, W. H., 11, 24, 39, 42, 45, 52
Hall, M. H., 25, 34
Hamilton, J., 45, 52
Hamilton, C. V., 4, 8, 20, 24
Hare, N., 5, 24
Hattem, J., 41, 53
Heine, R. W., 39, 41, 43, 44, 52
Hollingshead, A. B., 41, 52
Hughes, L., 24, 108
Hunter, D. M., 40, 52
James, O. C., 41, 53
Jefferson, E., 33
Johnson, L. B., 7
Kardiner, A., 39, 40, 52
Katz, W. L., 11, 24
Keniston, K. A., 25, 34
Kennedy, J. A., 43, 44, 52
Kerner, O., 11, 24
Kerr, N. G., v, vii, viii, 55–62
King, M. L., Jr., 6f
Klineberg, O., 39, 52
Kobler, F. J., vi
Lantz, E. M., 40, 53
Laskin, J., 28, 33, 34
Latimer, B. D., 3, 24
Louis, Joe, 15

Malcolm X., 58
Mayhew, L. B., 25, 34
Meredith, J., 7, 8
Mill, J. S., 59
Morris, W., 5, 24
Ovesey, L., 39, 40, 52
Owens, Jesse, 15
Parks, Rosa, 7, 8
Pugh, R. W., vi, 11, 14, 19, 24, 74
Redlich, F. C., 41, 52
Remond, Charles, 9
Robeson, Paul, 15
Rochester (see Anderson, E. "Rochester")
Rodgers, T. C., 45, 52
Rogers, C. R., 12, 24
Roosevelt, F. D., 87, 98
Rosen, H., 39, 41, 43, 52
Rosenthal, R., 38, 52
Rossman, M., 25, 34
St. Clair, H. R., 41, 43, 52
Sattler, J. M., 37, 38, 43, 44, 49, 52
Seward, G., 49, 52
Sommers, U. S., 43, 52
Spinoza, B., 59
Stanford, M., 26, 33, 34
Sterba, R., 45, 52
Thomas, A., 39, 52
Turner, N., 9
Waite, R., 43, 52
Walker, R. E., vi
Welcher, D. W., v
Wilson, D. C., 40, 53
Yamamoto, J., 41, 53

Subject Index

Abolitionist, 9
Activism
  black, v, 29, 31
  black student, v, 25ff
    categories of involvement, 27ff
    goals of, 32f
Activism (cont.)
  black-white student, 25ff
  civil rights, 25
  political, 33
  social, 60
  white student, 26ff
Adaptive inferiority, 10, 12, 13, 18, 19, 21, 23
Africa, 6, 107f
  Tembu of, 41
African(s), 5, 52, 105
African-Americans, 4

African culture, 41
African Methodist Episcopal (AME) Church, 18
Afro-Americans, 4, 105
Alcoholism, 40, 58
American Board of Professional Psychology, viii
American Council on Education, 14
Analysis, 47
  didactic, 39
Anxiety, 10ff, 20, 31, 32, 42, 43, 50, 51, 105
Anxiety conditioned to blackness, 10ff
Ardennes Campaign (the Battle of the Bulge), 98
Assumed superiority, 21
Atlanta University, 11
Attitudes, conscious and unconscious, 39
Attitude of Negroes Towards Negroes Scale, 14
Backlash, 21
Battlefield commission, 98
Behavior modification, 61 (*see also* Psychotherapy and Psychoanalysis)
Be-like-white success formula, 16, 31
Black bourgeoisie, 17, 106 (*see also* Black middle class)
Black community, 8, 31, 32f, 55ff, 105
  institutions, 59
Black consciousness, 26, 28
Black experience, 50, 69, 71, 72
  tragedy of, 66
Black ghetto, 59, 65
  Chicago southside, description of, 56f
  patients, description of population, 58
  urban, 17
Black liberation, 8f, 26, 27, 31, 32
"Black Maiden," poem by T. J. Edwards, 70
Black middle class, 17, 33, 60, 106 (*see also* Black bourgeoisie)
Black power, 60, 61
Black psychology, vi, 104–105

Black Revolution, v, 3–23, 25, 26, 27, 31, 107, 108
  birth of, 6ff
Black self-esteem, 31
Black Student Psychological Association, 31
Black-white relations, 20
Blues, the, 72
"Born Black," poem by T. J. Edwards, 69
Bourgeois standards, 50
Buzz bombs, 94
Change agent, 27
  social, 32
Chemotherapy, 58 (*see also* Drug therapy)
Chicago Tribune, 27, 34
Civil rights, 26, 28
  activism, 25
Clients
  black, 38ff, 42, 49ff (*see also* Black ghetto patients)
  white, 44ff
Clinical psychologists, v
Color-caste system, 12, 16, 30–31
Communism, 22, 71, 103
Community, academic, 29 (*see also* Black community)
Congruence, 10, 12
Control work, 39 (*see also* Psychoanalysis)
Corrective emotional learning, 11
Counseling, family, 61
Countertransference, 42, 44, 46 (*see also* Transference)
Crow-Jim phenomenon, 49 (*see also* Jim Crow)
Culture, African, 41
Defense (*see* Psychological defense)
Defensiveness, 71
  psychological, 66 (*see also* Psychological defense)
Discrimination, 43
Education
  liberal, 30
  of slaves, 11
Educational therapy, 61
Ego, 17, 40
  development, 44
Ego ideal, white, 40
Emancipation, 11

"Experiment," greatest social-psychological, 105
Experimenter bias, 51
Experimenter effects, racial, 37f
Fear of white man, 16
Fisk University, 13, 17
4050th Quartermaster Truck Company, Third U.S. Army, 96, 97
Freedom rides, 7, 19, 31
Ghetto, (*see* Black ghetto)
Growing up black, 65ff, 69, 72
Higher learning, institutions of
  integrated, 28f
  nonintegrated, black, 29ff
  white, 28f
History
  Afro-American, 105
  black man's, 29f
  of blacks, 9ff
Hypnotherapy, 61 (*see also* Therapy)
Identification, 45, 50
  with feces, 40
  with the aggressor, 10, 12, 23
Identity, 8, 20, 23, 61, 62, 105
  with the people, 59
Illinois Institute of Technology, 68
Inferiority, 13ff
  resignation to, 67
  status of, 67
  (*see also* Adaptive inferiority)
Integration game, 22
Iranian Ministry of Education, viii
Jackson State (College) incident, 33
Jim Crow, 66 (*see also* Crow-Jim phenomenon)
Johns Hopkins University, v
Kent State (University), 33
Ku Klux Klan, 11
Learning experience, 8
Liberation (*see* Black liberation)
Loyola University of Chicago, v, viii
Lynching, 16
  era of, 11

117

Lynch mob, 5
Malcolm X Shabazz Community Mental Health Center, Chicago, viii, 55, 57
Manteno State Hospital, viii, 55
March on Washington, 6ff
Mississippi, 7f
　University of, 7
Montgomery (Alabama) Bus Boycott, 7
"My Soul from out the Gloom of Bondage Cries," poem by R. W. Pugh, 96
Neurosis, 44
North Sea, 94ff
Northern Irish, 85
Northwestern University, 29, 33
Oedipal
　competition, 46
　material, 43
　transference, 46
Oedipus complex, 104
　(see also Oedipal)
Ohio State University, The, 74
Omaha Beachhead, 97
Paranoia, minority, 71
Personality, Negro, 39
Personality organization, 12
Political activism (see Activism)
Poor black, 57
　"untreatability of," 57
Psychoanalysis (see Analysis and Psychoanalytic)
Psychoanalysts, 45
Psychoanalytic
　literature, 39
　papers, 39
　session, 47
　training, 39
　writers, 39
Psychodrama, 61
Psychological
　processes, 5
　sabotage, 31
　scar tissue, 65, 66, 68, 71, 72
　stopgap measures, 12f
Psychological defense, 12f
　defensive patterns, 44
Psychologist, role of, 44ff, 57ff

Psychology of self-reclamation, 3ff, 20
Psychosexual problems, 70
Psychotherapist, 38ff, 45
　(see also Therapist)
Psychotherapy, v, 37ff, 51
　self-administered, 69
　(see also Therapy)
Queen Elizabeth, 84f
Race, psychology of, 38
Racial relations, 20ff
Racism, 8, 47
Reintegration, 5, 8
Reintegrative process, 5
Research with blacks, 14ff, 32, 37ff
Resistance, 21, 44, 45
Rhine, The, 98
Role, 20
　change, 21
　expectation, 21
　playing, 61
SDS (Students for a Democratic Society), 28
Self-acceptance, 8, 30
Self-actualization, self-actualizing, 3, 5, 8, 105, 108
Self-concept, 5, 8, 21
　(see also Self-esteem)
Self-devaluation, 5
Self-enhancement, 14
Self-esteem, 5, 23, 30, 32, 105, 106 (see also Self-concept)
Self-fulfilling prophecy, 10
Self-reclamation, psychology of, 3ff, 24
Self-rejection, 70
Self-system, 12
Self-worth, 10
Sense-of-self, 4, 5, 21
Sensitivity training, 61
SHAEF (Supreme Headquarters, Allied Expeditionary Force), 90, 98
Sit-ins, 7
　lunch counter, 26
Slave(s), 6, 10, 105
　education of, 11
　ex-slave, 17
　Negro, 40
Social change agent, 32
Somatic delusion, 48
Song of Solomon, 18

State University of New York (SUNY), viii
Stereotype, 3, 7
　racial, 41
　whitey's, 68
Stereotypic behavior, 67
Student Nonviolent Coordinating Committee (SNCC), 26f
Students
　black, 26
　white, 26
Superiority (see Assumed superiority)
Temple University, viii
Testing, diagnostic, 32, 37, 61
Therapeutic relationship, 38ff, 59
Therapist, 38ff, 43
　black, 44ff
　white, 38ff
Therapy, 38ff
　drug, 42
　(see also Chemotherapy)
　educational, 61
　hypno-, 61
　social-action, 61
　work, 61
　(see also Psychotherapy)
Third U.S. Army, 96, 97
Transference, 42, 45, 48
　hostile, 43
　oedipal, 46
　phenomena, 45
Trauma, racial, 71
Uncle Tom, 50
University of Chicago, 56
University of Detroit, viii
Variables
　client, 42ff, 50f
　subject, 38
　therapist, 38ff, 48ff
Wayne State University, viii
We-ain't-ready syndrome, 13
White culture, 30
White power structure, 31, 33
White racism, 5, 29, 32
Whites, "radical," 30
World War I, 11
World War II, 16, 21ff, 31, 71, 73ff
　D Day, 97